WALLAROO 19

CELEBRATING WOMEN'S RUGBY IN AUSTRALIA

LIBBY ANDREW

First published by Ultimate World Publishing 2024
Copyright © 2024 Libby Andrew

ISBN

Paperback - 978-1-923255-42-5
Ebook - 978-1-923255-43-2

Libby Andrew has asserted her rights under the Copyright, Designs and Patents Act 1988 to be identified as the author of this work. The information in this book is based on the author's experiences and opinions. The publisher specifically disclaims responsibility for any adverse consequences which may result from use of the information contained herein. Permission to use information has been sought by the author. Any breaches will be rectified in further editions of the book.

All rights reserved. No part of this publication may be reproduced, stored in or introduced into a retrieval system, or transmitted in any form, or by any means (electronic, mechanical, photocopying, recording or otherwise) without the prior written permission of the author. Any person who does any unauthorised act in relation to this publication may be liable to criminal prosecution and civil claims for damages. Enquiries should be made through the publisher.

Cover design: Ultimate World Publishing
Layout and typesetting: Ultimate World Publishing
Editor: James Salmon

Ultimate World Publishing
Diamond Creek,
Victoria Australia 3089
www.writeabook.com.au

DISCLAIMER

To the best of my ability, memory and resources, this is my personal account of the history, including the games of women's rugby league, women's rugby sevens and women's rugby union in Australia from the year 1991.

I am an imperfect human, so please excuse me if I have made any errors, especially if I have misspelt someone's name or neglected to include someone whose name I really wanted to include but have forgotten.

TESTIMONIALS

"I'm proud to say I got the ball rolling in Lib's football career! I knew Lib and her family from our time in St Jude's Parish in Canberra. We went to the same primary and secondary schools and university, and both played netball in the local Arawang District competition. I signed up for Canberra's first women's rugby league competition after seeing a newspaper ad calling for players. We were looking to get more players into the fledgling competition, and I just knew Lib was the perfect fit, so I asked her at uni, and again at netball, if she'd like to come along and have a go. She was hesitant at first but I persevered and drove her to her first game in Belconnen. Of course Lib smashed it - the first ball she received she just tucked it under her arm, burst through the defence and stormed to the try line. We'd found a winner in Lib and our East Canberra side went on to win many competitions with her in the side. And to reflect now on what she achieved as a pioneer for women's rugby league and union, and on the world rugby stage, is just mind-blowing!"

Helen Cross (Wylks)
East Canberra WRL, ACTWRL, Canberra Royals Wallaroos,
ACTWRU

"My rugby journey started as a seven-year-old watching five brothers play backyard footy in Gisborne, NZ. A few years later, I joined my primary school rugby team, where I was the only girl in the team. I was hurling myself at anything moving on the field. I think for most kids growing up in NZ, at some point in your life you had played netball, rugby, softball or hockey. Sadly, I was never good with a stick in my hand and hit everything but the ball. But put a football in my hand, and that was another story! Whilst I was exposed to many sports, my fascination, love, and of course a cheeky determination to outperform my five brothers was always in rugby! When I turned 10, my family moved to Australia, and unfortunately, there was no pathway for girls playing rugby in Oz. So, it was back to the netball courts, softball pitch and backyard cricket with the neighbours.

Several years on, I finally got the opportunity to play touch football in Canberra. It wasn't rugby but close enough! I was that crazy, little Maori girl side-stepping, swerving, cut-passing and dummy-switching her way up the field. Within a few short games of touch I realised how much I was drawn to the adrenalin rush – and how that had been missing in all the other sports I played. So, you can imagine my excitement when at the age of 24, I was asked to help pull together the first ever women's rugby team in Canberra to compete at the Nationals. I had no idea where this journey would take me. All I knew was that I was bursting at the seams with excitement, anticipation and passion to play rugby.

Now aged 54, and happily married with two beautiful girls (well three, including my wife), I feel so honoured and privileged to have gone on this journey, as one of the pioneers for women in contact sport in Australia. My life has been enriched in ways that are beyond words. I am forever grateful for all the incredible people, and lifelong rugby friends that I have met along the way. Thank you Lib for all the memories we've shared, and those wild and crazy times overseas, in Canberra, and Sydney throughout our 30-year friendship…Glad you kept some of those "What happens on tour, stays on tour…" out of your book lol!"

Louise Ferris-Taylor
Wallaroo #9

"As if East Canberra Women's Rugby League Team in 1991 wasn't hard enough to play against…then Libby Andrew joins the team! I played rugby league with and against Lib from 1991 to 1994, much preferring that she was on my team! Lib had a low centre of gravity making her hard to tackle and she was tough in attack and defence, a very competitive and talented player. Lib had a wide smile and cheeky laugh, tough as nails and enjoyed a good time.

I caught up with her again in 1999 (Australian Women's Rugby League National Championships) and then not until her delayed 50th birthday celebrations in October 2022. They say true friends remain the same, and this is spot on with Lib. Same wide smile, cheeky laugh, toughness and commitment but a gentle, genuine friend. A catch up with Lib wipes the years of absence away and time is irrelevant.

Congratulations Lib on celebrating 30 years of women's rugby union. Your passion for the sport, love of rugby and its culture, commitment to being the best you can be, and involvement (and memories) not only during your playing years but into the future, are a credit to who you are."

Cath Welch
Foundation Member #1, Australian Women's Rugby League Team (Inaugural player and captain), played in first Jillaroos Team for Australia 1996, ACT rep, Rams player

"Libby Andrew was a pioneer of women's rugby (union) not only in the ACT, but Australia. She was also one of our best players as a fierce tackling, hard running backrower and Wallaroo #19. Libby and her early colleagues from 1992 were the 'true believers' of the women's game in this country and despite indifference, suspicion, sabotage and at times outright misogyny, they persisted and today's players owe them a great debt. The women's game of rugby has come a long way since those early days of 1992 and while equality has not yet been achieved, the finish line is at least in sight.

The book is a great read and historically important in accurately documenting that often told story of ordinary people achieving extraordinary things that leave a lasting legacy."

Dougal Whitton
Canberra Royals Women's & Men's Coach and ACT Women's & Schoolboys Coach Canberra Royals and ACT player

"Libby Andrew has written an important and inspiring memoir that follows the nascent days of women's rugby union in Australia.

The book is a testament to Libby's contribution, her dedication, commitment and downright tenaciousness in following her dream to represent Australia in the sport she loved.

The book spares no detail and offers inspiring stories that share the highs and lows and that added to Libby's already strong character.

I met Libby when she became a police officer in the Northern Territory and in this endeavour again her dedication and commitment was a shining light to others.

Libby's memoir brings you close to an inspiring journey that makes you wish you had been part of it. Libby was always meant to write this story and the evidence is there in the reading."

Kate Vanderlaan APM
Ex NT Police, close friend, colleague and gym buddy

"Libby has written a wonderful book about her time playing rugby back in an era when there were a lot of hurdles for females playing a male-dominated sport.

I met Libby around 1996 when we were playing for our respective states at the Nationals, before we both went on to make the Wallaroos squad. We were also in the inaugural team to represent our country at the Hong Kong 7s, though we could not go as Australia as we were not sanctioned by Australian Rugby (one of those hurdles I mentioned).

Libby always gave 100% effort in games and was one of the toughest competitors on the field both physically and mentally. She never made it easy for her opposition. She worked hard on her fitness and maintained a high level through her playing years whether it was 7s or 15-a-side; a wonderful athlete.

Lib is a bit of a character, lots of laughs when we get to catch up, also up for a dare now and then. I am privileged to have been a part of Libby's rugby journey and I am also privileged to have been asked to write a testimonial for her book. Thanks mate for sharing your story and some of the history of women's rugby along the way."

Tanya "Ozzie" Osborne
Wallaroo #37

"Libby's book captivated me. I am Wallaroo cap #45, and this read and the memories certainly got my rugby juices running. I first knew of Libby when I was the half back for Queensland and she was playing flanker for the ACT Brumbies at the 1996 Nationals. We were both part of the first Australian Women's World Cup Wallaroos Team and I also played 7s Rugby with Libby for the Australian (Aussie Gold) team in Hong Kong (1999 and 2000).

Her easy-to-read story brought back the early struggles for recognition but mostly the elation which came with being called a Wallaroo! These memories are so easily forgotten so I applaud Libby for being so brave and courageous to document her story and the history-making beginnings of women's rugby in Australia.

Libby, like me, was one of the fittest people in women's rugby, tenacious, dedicated, and strong. I preferred being on the same team as Libby and not her opposition! We all just soaked up any skills and experience in those early days so we could be the best. Libby's contribution to rugby at all levels has been an example of the highest degree. I have made the most wonderful friends playing rugby and there is something about rugby girls. They are all like family - they just have your back always. We have regular catch-ups in Queensland through the Vintage Reds (women who have represented Queensland Reds from 1996) and now it's so great to have the Classic Wallaroos (women who have represented Australia since its inception in 1993).

Libby has done a great job documenting these first ten years of women's rugby in Australia. She is a real pioneer of our sport. I just wished I was living in this era of women's sport and the opportunities they have today."

Karen Bucholz
Wallaroo #45

"Libby Andrew's memoir is a captivating narrative that delves deep into our shared journey in women's rugby. From the exhilarating rush of our inaugural test match as Black Ferns against the Wallaroos, to the intense battles of international competitions, Libby's storytelling vividly captures the essence of our collective struggles and triumphant moments on the pitch. Her unwavering dedication to preserving the rich history of women's rugby permeates every page, serving as a poignant reminder of the challenges we faced and the victories we celebrated. As someone who stood alongside Libby on the rugby field and cherishes our friendship, I am profoundly grateful for her enduring commitment to the sport and her remarkable ability to inspire others through her words. Libby's memoir stands as a powerful testament to the resilience and camaraderie that define women's rugby, making it an indispensable read for athletes and enthusiasts alike. With each chapter, she masterfully weaves personal anecdotes with broader themes of perseverance, teamwork, and the relentless pursuit of excellence, offering invaluable insights into the profound impact of rugby on our lives."

Louisa Wall
Black Fern #59

"I had the pleasure, and the challenge of playing against and alongside Lib. We were combatants in the first National Championships final in 1996, and teammates for the Wallaroos and the Aussie Gold 7s shortly after. In these early years as we played our hearts out on suburban fields we had no idea we were 'trailblazers' or that one day women would play before sell-out crowds. We loved the game and just wanted to play it at every opportunity we got.

Like Libby I have invested energy in documenting the history of those early days. In 2021 I documented the history of every woman who had worn the treasured maroon representing Queensland Rugby, celebrating the occasion by presenting almost 150 of them with their honour caps on a single day. I assisted New South Wales in documenting their women's history shortly after. I treasure the opportunities to work with the Queensland Vintage Red to celebrate past players and invest in the future stars. The journey from the early days of one-size-fits-all uniforms, to mentoring the current crop of stars, is one that continues to be immensely rewarding. To everyone who has contributed to this journey, as coach, player, administrator, or a flexible employer, the women's game continues to grow, face, and overcome challenges because of you. In this book Libby tells the story of her journey, a journey I shared for many years and one we're immensely proud of."

Vanessa Bradley (Nottenboom)
Wallaroo #40

"A fascinating insight into the "real pioneers" of the rugby codes (league & union) for women in this country. A story about "true trailblazers" - their adventures, struggles and triumphs that have largely gone unrecorded. This book is a beautiful reminder that the "little things" are often as special as the big."

Matt O'Connor
Wallaby #713

"This book provides an authentic look at Libby's rugby journey and the many people she has met during her journey. It covers the highs, the lows, the sacrifices required, and the rugby "roller coaster" ride that many women have experienced in Australia.

Even though we have both retired from playing the game and dealing with the pre-match atmosphere (including the smell of Dencorub, the silent or noisy preparations of some players, and various rituals and rants), the one thing that will always remain are the lifelong friendships that were made. I count Libby as one of those lifelong friendships.

The passion and fundamentals for women's rugby remains high for so many trailblazers such as Libby. They have left 'footprints' to ensure the game continues to evolve for females in all levels of the game.

A big thank you to Libby for trusting me to write some words for your book. I am honoured to be a small part of your rugby journey and your life."

Shirley Russell
Wallaroo #26

"As yet I've not met Libby in person, we met through a Zoom meeting we both attended, since then a friendship has grown up by frequently using this medium.

It's been a pleasure and privilege to proofread her book from its inception to the final draft.

Oh what a journey it's been, as a Pom my knowledge of Australian words has greatly increased and many chuckles, along with some banter about our two countries, friendly of course!

Through our chats and reading this book only reinforces what I know about Libby, she has an insatiable zest for life, and an incredible drive to achieve everything she does to the highest standard. She has a big heart, a wild sense of humour, a determination to have her voice, and that of women, heard, yet she is kind, gentle and an amazing mum to her four boys.

I look forward to travelling to Canberra one day when I'm visiting my daughter in Adelaide to finally meet Libby, it's a journey I anticipate with great joy in my heart.

Libby's book is a validation of her love of sport, rugby (both codes) and for the voice of women's rugby union in Australia to be heard, acknowledged and hopefully gain parity with the men's game in the near future.

I make this point as during our discussions this has been a recurring and very strong theme, something she is very passionate about, and rightly so.

Thanks, Libby, for the journey, education, and laughter both late at night and early in the morning! It's been a blast."

Phyll Buckley
Pommy mate #1

I was a Sports Trainer with the Woden Valley Rams Rugby League Club when the Rams female side commenced playing in 1991. We were very lucky at the time to have Peter Cox, in charge. When I suggested the ladies needed to be afforded the same "medical" standards, ie, strapping and trainers, as the men, he agreed. I got the job of being their Sports Trainer for the season.

I was still a Sports Trainer with the men when I noticed that the women kept turning up to train, but the Coach did not, maybe something to do with the lack of wins they were having. I thought then that this was a very determined bunch and giving up was not an option. This went on for a couple of nights and I could resist no longer, and I still remember the night. I went over to the girls and said something like, "I'm only a sports trainer, not a coach, but I have played the game, and I might be able to show you a couple of things". They gladly accepted and the journey begun, and I am forever grateful it did.

As part of that journey, I got to meet and know Libby. There was always one consistent, no matter the situation, her smile. Not an ordinary smile, a mischievous smile like she was about to get up to something, and she usually was. Libby was a fierce competitor, and she loved the game and could play the game well. Libby also loved the after-game functions. Those were the days when players would compete fiercely on the field and party together like there was no tomorrow afterwards. I've spent many a day and many such evenings with Libby those early years.

The Women in those early days were fierce competitors but also strong ally's where no problem that presented itself could not be solved. I'm sure this book has given the readers an insight into the tenacity, the toughness, and the resolve of these early pioneers which Libby Andrew is one. I am both proud and delighted that she has chosen to share her journey in print.

John Squizzy Taylor
Player, Sports Trainer, Coach and National Selector

DEDICATION

Alice Cooper, Sue Dorrington, Mary Forsyth and Deborah Griffin made up the Organising Committee of the first ever Women's Rugby World Cup (Wales 1991). I dedicate this book to these four amazing ladies and thank you for not only a successful first WRWC but for the effort and sacrifices you made for all women to join this sport and play in subsequent WRWC's around the globe. I believe the 1991 WRWC placed some pressure on the Australian Rugby Union to "get the ball rolling" in Australia. Without your efforts, I may have missed the opportunity to play. I feel grateful to you all.

CONTENTS

Disclaimer	iii
Testimonials	v
Dedication	xv
Foreword	xix
Introduction	1
Ode to Joan Forno	3
In memory of Robert (Bob) Hitchcock	9
In memory of Mieke Jane Fortune (nee Gladwin)	13
1. Admit One	15
2. Warm Up	29
3. League Came First	39
4. Newcastle, NSW	55
5. First International Test	85
6. 1995 – 1997	93
7. Wallaroos First World Cup 1998	109
8. A Truckload of 15s and 7s Rugby	125
9. League Versus Union	161
10. Learnings	171
11. Leaving My Footprint	185
12. Career Timelines	191
Glossary	201
Afterword	203
About the Author	205
Acknowledgements	207
References	209
Honour Roll	211

FOREWORD

It is an absolute honour to be asked to write the foreword in this book written by Libby Andrew, Wallaroo #19. This book is an insight into someone who has a passion to succeed, whether it was in other sports, rugby or in life generally. I must express my gratitude to Libby for her contribution to the team and the sport, and recognise her role in shaping the history of the Wallaroos. For having the courage to document her thoughts, relive the good and somewhat hard times experienced by the first Wallaroo's, and their achievements since the first Development Squad was selected in Newcastle in 1993.

Women's rugby in Australia has a rich and storied history that has often been overshadowed by the more widely recognised men's game. In this groundbreaking book by Libby, we delve into the untold stories of the pioneering women and men who have shaped the sport and paved the way for future generations.

From humble beginnings in 1994 when the Wallaroos played their first international Women's Rugby Union Test Match at the North Sydney Oval against the New Zealand Black Ferns, where we learnt quickly that to be the best on the international stage we would have to work much harder to play this game called rugby union, and better understand what we had to achieve if we wanted to be on the bright lights of international competition. The journey of women's rugby in Australia is one of resilience, determination, and triumph. Through interviews, archival research, and firsthand accounts, we uncover the challenges and triumphs faced by female players, coaches, management, and administrators as they fought for recognition and respect in a traditionally male-dominated sport.

This book celebrates the courage and tenacity of the women who have blazed a trail for others to follow and shines a light on the remarkable achievements and contributions of female rugby players in Australia. It is a testament to the power of passion, perseverance, and teamwork in overcoming obstacles and achieving greatness, and Libby has captured so many of the struggles that both she and each player involved encountered to achieve their goals of playing this sport.

Looking to the future growth of women's rugby, and especially the national team, the Wallaroos, if the opportunity arises to play, support, sponsor every young girl or lady, they deserve that opportunity to be part of this great sport.

Whether you are a die-hard rugby fan or simply curious about the history of women's sports, this book offers a fascinating and inspiring look at the evolution of women's rugby in Australia. So, join me on this journey as we pay tribute to the trailblazers, the game-changers, and the unsung heroes of women's rugby in Australia. Libby's stories deserve to be told, and the legacy of women's rugby deserves to be celebrated.

Joan Forno
Inaugural President of the Australian Women's Rugby Union

INTRODUCTION

This book reflects my own personal history while playing women's rugby union in Australia. My rugby journey started with the first women's rugby challenge in Newcastle, New South Wales, in 1992. It ended 10 years later at the completion of the 2002 Women's Rugby World Cup, Barcelona, Spain.

The purpose of writing this book is to leave my own footprint. Those years were just too damn good to be kept locked inside my head and the dusty treasure chest lying dormant in my garage.

I hope you will learn something about the history of women's rugby union in Australia and maybe enjoy a laugh or two along the way. Historically, women's rugby has come and gone across the globe, in fits and starts, sometimes with one off fundraising games or charity matches in the 1920s and 1930s, again in the 1950s and 1980s. The same has been true here in Australia. For a multitude of reasons, history of the women's game, copies of sign on sheets and even match results have been difficult to locate. I didn't want this to happen during my era. This history forms a decade of my adult life and some amazing learnings and experiences.

My very first game of rugby union was as a player in a team called the Canberra Royals Wallaroos. We travelled to NSW and participated in what became the beginning of this new era of women's rugby in Australia. Consistently, the women's game has been played every year in Australia since 1992. Equality in the game of rugby is changing, and it has been amazing to not only be a part of that history but to witness growth of the women's game.

Historically, rugby union, along with many other codes of male-dominated contact sports were considered a man's game. In this 21st century, rugby union has expanded to include girls at the grassroots level and adult women players. Aussie women are celebrating their inclusion into a sport, not only these days on the paddocks around the globe but in coaching, refereeing, administration and various other roles which were predominantly also reserved for men. I thank God for this change and for the opportunity that rugby has brought into my life.

I played rugby because I love the game, the challenges, the mates and the whole cultural package. I never played to prove anything to anyone aside from the opposition, whom I really wanted to defeat.

I timed self-publishing this book with the 30-year anniversary of the first international women's rugby union Test Match in Australia. This not only gives me a great pleasure on this milestone but ticks another item off my bucket list.

ODE TO JOAN FORNO

On Saturday, the 6th of June, 1992, Joan Forno first introduced herself to the Canberra Royals Wallaroos Team at the Newcastle Challenge. In true Joan style, she approached the team on the grassy paddock and started organising us, ensuring that we all knew where we needed to be and what time the safety session would commence. This was day one, during the morning of the inaugural Women's Rugby Challenge, Newcastle.

Joan had a presence everywhere she went. At every tournament she was involved with, she was deeply involved and highly committed to ensuring that whatever it was, it was organised, prepared and conducted to the best of her ability. Joan's commitment to women's rugby union in this country has been and always will be outstanding and beyond measure.

At the 1992 inaugural Challenge, Joan was listed as a coach of a team called P.M.T (which stood for Pretty Magnificent Tarts). Joan was interviewed by John Laws (2UE Radio King) as to why women wanted to play rugby. Her response was a simple "WHY NOT"! Joan remains an advocate of our game. She believed that it was time for women to get out of the spectator stands and onto the paddock.

It seemed to me, that very first weekend arriving in Newcastle, Joan Forno believed she was "coach" of all five women's teams, not just the P.M.T. Blues. Joan was everywhere that weekend, organising everything and introducing herself to everyone. This included about 75 clueless women's players, Ray

Lewis the director, Gerry and Justin who were the announcers, Peter Saunders the grounds manager, the registrar, the first aid volunteers, and even those four adorable young ball girls (Karlee Scott, Simone Peacock, Jessica Morgan and Madelin Worrad). Apparently, we all needed bossing! Joan was in her element. She is magical to sit back and watch.

Over that weekend, Joan Forno possibly had dealings with every single player. It was easy to see that Joan was a born organiser and this tournament meant a lot to her. Our team dubbed Joan with the nickname "Nana" because of the style of eyeglasses worn in 1992 (and because she was as beautiful as the Greek singer and politician Nana Mouskouri). We all loved Joan. Kind of in the way you might love your own mother and fear her at the same time!

It was clear that Joan loved rugby as much as we loved playing it. Everywhere Joan went, husband Allan was in tow too. A truly amazing and dedicated couple to the game of women's rugby, men's rugby and especially the Golden Oldies too.

A side note, when we could not find a women's team to train against, it was a quick call to Allan Forno who would rustle together members of a Golden Oldies Team wherever we were training and a group of "mature aged men" would appear and help us. We were also lucky to have the then Australian Rugby front row Phil Kearns, Ewan McKenzie and Tony Daley, winger David Campese, fullback Matt Burke come and give us their insight on to how we could better play our positions.

Joan went from coach in 1992, to the inaugural president of women's rugby union for Australia in 1993. She was so well connected in the rugby circles everywhere and worldwide too. We all always did what Joan requested (and this was not limited to players only, I am pretty sure that coaches and other managers jumped accordingly as well). Leo Williams, the chairman of the ARU, made the smartest decision ever, appointing Joan Forno to kick start rugby in Australia for women. I doubt whether there would be another human capable of doing what Joan Forno did for women's rugby in Australia.

ODE TO JOAN FORNO

Joan's commitment to our game never wavered. In 1994 she was present when we played our first international match in Sydney – no doubt she was responsible for making this event happen. In 1997 when we appeared at the Women's Rugby Hong Kong Sevens, Joan was our manager and the surrogate mother, attending to everything (including coaching)! 12 months later in 1998 in our first appearance at the International World Cup in Holland, Joan was our team manager again. She worked tirelessly during the tournaments and no doubt for weeks and months behind the scenes writing letters, trying to find sponsors and fulfilling the endless duties of a volunteer.

On behalf of the entire Wallaroos family, from the inaugural Newcastle Challenge to the internationals Test series, the World Cups, the Hong Kong Sevens, we will always be super grateful to you for it all.

Without the hard work, dedication, and contacts that Joan (and husband Allan) both had, I doubt whether we would have ever made that 1998 World Cup in Holland. It may have at least taken another four years for someone less capable and connected to get us organised and to convince the ARU that we were ready. Only Joan will ever know the work that was required.

The 1992 tournament in Newcastle, so we thought at the time, was a one-off. We returned to Canberra where there was no competition for us to continue to play. Sadly we all went our separate ways. Unbeknownst to us, Mrs Joan Forno was hard at work behind the scenes, already preparing for the tournament to be repeated the following year in 1993. This inaugural year of rugby union would be the start of a new beginning for women's sport in Australia. The tournament would continue annually, and it seemed that rugby union for women was finally here to stay.

What I know about Joan (which may not be the full story) includes;

1993 – Inaugural President of the Australian Women's Rugby Union

1993 – First female rep to the Australian Rugby Union Council and meetings

1994 – Responsible for the first international Test between Australia and NZ

1995 – Chaired the first Australian Women's Advisory Committee meeting

1995 – Part of the touring squad to New Zealand for the first official trip

1996 – Fighting to keep us going when funding was limited and sponsors nowhere to be seen. No matter what we needed somehow Joan managed to secure it, whether it was borrowed, purloined, or just fell into our kit bags, you knew everything would be covered! Our first ever real sponsors were Ford.

1997 – Hong Kong Sevens, Aussie Gold Team Manager

1998 – World Cup Team Manager in Holland (youngest team to be registered) and to be able to participate we had to have played one Test match against another IRB country to be eligible to enter. This was the game against New Zealand Black Ferns in Dunedin in August of 1997.

1999 – Hong Kong Sevens, Aussie Gold Team Manager

2000 – Hong Kong Sevens, Aussie Gold Team Manager

2000 – Joan was awarded the Australian Medal for her services to women's rugby

2001 – Hong Kong Sevens, Aussie Gold Team Manager

2015 – First female recipient of the Joe French Award for services to Australian rugby union and women's rugby.

Joan stepped down from her role as the president of Australian Women's Rugby in 2001 (and is still recovering and no doubt giggling) from the experience. Women's rugby in this country will forever be indebted to this amazing, kind, generous and highly capable lady. Thank you, Joan.

ODE TO JOAN FORNO

Joan Forno & Bob Hitchcock

IN MEMORY OF ROBERT (BOB) HITCHCOCK

Bob was a highly respected and well-loved man. This was not restricted to the rugby clubs and associations throughout Queanbeyan and Canberra, but Australia and internationally too. He devoted his life to the game of rugby. He was a gentleman, a husband, father, grandfather, friend, coach and mentor to literally thousands of players!

Bob was a player, coach, selector, mentor, committee member and vice president. Having graduated as a schoolteacher, Bob coached numerous junior and senior club teams, ACT senior representative teams and the Australian Under-21s. He was appointed the inaugural coach of the 1990 Emerging Wallabies team that included the likes of John Eales, David Willson, Willie Ofahengaue and Jason Little. The Wallabies went on to win the Rugby World Cup in the following year. He was passionate about developing talent identification and development programs for players.

Many people like Bob, who devote so much of their lives to a game they love, do so as volunteers. Bob was no different. He was involved because he loved sharing his knowledge, assisting others to achieve their best and being a part of the worldwide rugby family.

His efforts and passion for coaching culminated with a paid role at the Australian Institute of Sport firstly as Manager of Elite Programs then a brief appointment as CEO in the lead-up to the 2000 Olympics. Bob also ran the rugby scholarship program (which at that stage was restricted to male players only) at the Australian Institute of Sport, Canberra from its inception until 1995. He developed the Level 3 Coaching Program and was an accredited trainer for the International Rugby Board.

Upon his retirement from paid employment, or so he thought, he stepped into the women's game and repeated this same commitment again. He wasn't done yet and perhaps the best for our "Bobby" was yet to come. Bob shared his last rugby chapter of his life with "his girls". He coached the Women's National Team (Wallaroos) and took us to our first World Cup in the Netherlands. Bob was also the first coach of the Australian Women's Sevens Rugby Team, touring Hong Kong in 1997. By 2002 Bob was "trying" to step away from the huge commitment from rugby but had one more Women's Rugby World Cup in him. He was Assistant Coach of the Wallaroos, his very last tour (Spain 2002). His rugby biography could fill a whole book and the impression he left on his team and all members is long lasting. We all loved Bob.

Bob was formally recognised for his contribution to rugby in the NSW / ACT region and was awarded Life Membership of the ACT and Southern NSW Rugby Union. He was further named in the ACT Sport Hall of Fame in 2012 and was a recipient of the Medal of the Order of Australia. His legacy in rugby was embodied in 2018 (locally in Canberra) with the Bob Hitchcock Territory Shield introduced into the John Dent I Cup competition. He has been awarded Life Member status with both Queanbeyan and the ACT Rugby Unions.

IN MEMORY OF ROBERT (BOB) HITCHCOCK

Libby Andrew & Bob Hitchcock

IN MEMORY OF MIEKE JANE FORTUNE (NEE GLADWIN)

Mieke arrived on the Australian women's rugby scene with a forceful hit! No one could ignore this giant-sized, tall, athletic, smiling athlete. Mieke had this amazingly friendly and beautiful presence. She was genuine. She played and trained hard and knew how to party all night too. Even before arriving on the rugby scene, Mieke had achieved great things in various other sports but her presence at the Queensland University campus was timed perfectly with the progression of women's rugby union in Australia. Mieke arrived at the 1996 Australian Women's Nationals proudly wearing the maroon jersey and representing her state of Queensland. Her representative rugby went from playing for Queensland Uni, to the Queensland Reds and the Australian Wallaroos. Mieke made her test debut as lock in the 1996 test against the Black Ferns, Sydney and went on to play a total of ten tests for Australia.

Mieke and Lisa Dwan were a strong and solid unit that, on the field, travelled everywhere together. They were an amazingly tough and highly competitive second row who both went on to become the powerhouse in the centre of the Wallaroo scrum and lineout. They were both effective on the field in play too, dominating the opposition worldwide (apart from the Kiwis)!

Mieke is the only female member of our Wallaroo players team to have passed from this life and made it to rugby heaven thus far. On the 8th of August, 2018, Mieke lost her battle with breast cancer and left behind a gaping hole in our hearts and lives. Mieke left behind an amazingly high standard for any Australian lock to attempt to match, including a legacy and memories that will never be forgotten. She is and will always be a true-blue mate to those fortunate enough to have known and loved her.

Mieke and I both retired from rugby after our final game against Scotland at the 2002 World Cup, Spain. Along with hubby Graham, she visited my home in the backyard of the police complex at Yuendumu, NT. We spent some time exploring the bush and wandering around, her wearing those familiar gaiters (and because she was always very practical too)! Mieke and Graham, during rugby retirement, went on to operate and own a successful wholesale horticultural business on the Sunshine Coast. Three beautiful children were also a product of this amazing human being and family, who will never, ever be forgotten. Rest in peace mate, we all look forward to sharing a beer with you when and if we also make it to your resting place.

One of Mieke's daughters, Meg J Fortune, is 17 years old and is already proving her athletic ability as an exciting utility player for both 7s and 15s rugby union in Queensland. We hope to see Meg running around in the green and gold very soon.

Nic, Bron, Mieke & Lib (1998)

ADMIT ONE

On Monday, 2nd of September, 2024, women across our nation, especially members of the Australian Wallaroos' extended rugby family, will be celebrating. The occasion is 30 years since our very first women's international Test Match in Sydney. The ARU are planning a women's Test Match and function for Wallaroos past and present to celebrate and enjoy.

I invite you to join me on a journey through the pages of this book. I have compiled a personal reflection of the first decade, of the story from one player's perspective of Australian women's rugby union. I was there, but just to clarify; this book is not intended to contain my autobiography, rather just an overview of a very important and special decade of my life.

The Australian Women's National Rugby Union Team played against the New Zealand National Women's Team at North Sydney Oval on Friday evening, 2nd September, 1994. New Zealand (NZ) were the standout winners, final score 37-0.

On the night of that first test, we fronted as a team resembling joeys more than wallaroos. We sported our first ever rugby nappies, dummies and tried hard to hold possession of the Gilbert against a fierce and well-drilled opposition. The Kiwi girls were brutal and in true tradition of our Anzac friends, the match was intense. Our inexperience and lack of match fitness was obvious, but we tried our hardest and never gave up. We were just no match for these NZ women who, by the way, had been playing rugby for 20 years before we got started in Australia.

Although the score is always relevant and, in this case, historic, Australia had finally made it to the international women's rugby arena. It was a beginning. It had taken years, many stoppages and plenty of trying, but we finally ran onto the field that evening, wearing the green and gold and had the privilege of singing our National Anthem. I don't really think any of our team realised what a big deal that first international match was, given the long history of rugby in this country and worldwide.

Sir William Webb-Ellis is known worldwide as the creator of rugby union (1823). If Emily Valentine was in fact the first young woman to be given permission to play rugby in a team with her brothers in Northern Ireland (1887), the Australian women's team had some catching up to do. We were 107 years behind, not to mention that we weren't colonised for 99 of those years! Either way, women worldwide were excited that the first Australian women's rugby union team had stepped into the arena, though possibly not as excited as I was. This was the ultimate.

This book is a celebration of our women's rugby union journey in the land down under. What I experienced during the first ten years of the 2nd phase of women's rugby in our nation was an amazing and fun-filled journey. It is my absolute privilege and pleasure to finally get this book published.

This Australian Women's Rugby Union Team of 1994 included: Amanda Lingwood, Pearl Palaialii, Bronwyn Calvert, Angela Doidge, Tina Chapman, Robyn Chambers, Kerry Davis, Kathy Beitzel, Deena Aitken, Libby Andrew, Nicki Wickert, Margie Shelley, Yasmin Stafford, Bronwen

ADMIT ONE

Hart, Angel McGurgen, Sharyn Williams, Julianne Columbus, Louise Ferris, Karla Clay, Ronnie May, Helen Taylor (Captain), Angela Fairweather (Vice Captain) and Selena Worsley.

We were supported by: Mrs Joan Forno (President of Women's Rugby Union), Mr Jack Scott (Chairman), Mick Willis (Coach), Paul Cornish (Assistant Coach), and Christine (Goldie) Gold (Manager).

1994 Team and Management (September 1994)

The official team photo along with a few other gems can be found throughout these pages. My surname appears with an 's' after the Andrew in some publications which continues to be a temptation for people. Sometimes my name appears as Elizabeth, other times Libby, but my truest mates call me Lib. It is my intention to attempt to get the spelling of my teammates correct in these pages. Apologies, in advance, if I have made any errors.

I also thank the Lord that our "footy fashion" has progressed over the past 30 years! The playing strip in the early days consisted of the "off cuts" or spares of the men's kit which were tossed to the women's team to save money. It was standard to see some of those short, skinny, backline players wearing a jersey that could house the entire back line. If the jersey was tucked into the playing shorts, it would be seen hanging out the bottom of the shorts. Sadly, this was not only limited to our Aussie girls but to other nations too.

During my playing career, I felt grateful for a 2XXL jersey that was green and gold and had some form of logo. Although it was sad and the early years' jerseys were rarely a proper fit, we were happy to be granted permission to play rugby. The jersey colour, sizes, logos, our team's name, the tracksuits and even our identity would all be challenged in the years which I reflect over in this book.

You may notice our first international team photo within these pages. We were not given a choice to wear those full-length skirts and stockings. This uniform was reserved for the official team functions. Those of us selected in subsequent years would be asked to "bring the good kit back" (better known as our #1s!) as we would be required to wear the same formal kit in subsequent years (to save money as the women's budget has always been tight).

This is the kit we were photographed in for that first official team photo (and in subsequent years there were other extraordinary skirts and apparel). That first year we were even given a makeup kit and a lady's wallet. We were and remain grateful for it all.

Our dress up gear worn away from the rugby field was known to the squad as our "number #1". During 1994, this included these large hanky-like garments tied around our necks. Few of us knew how to tie it (let alone wear this garment) and prior to 1994, a hanky was something in my pocket or tucked inside my bra, good for blowing my nose, helping to stop a bleed or wiping away tears. These large and silky hankies were not only bulky and embarrassing to wear but were bloody uncomfortable and awkward too (just my opinion). I never felt right in the number #1 attire. In fact, I've always felt awkward in a skirt or dress of any kind. I prefer to wear it for the shortest possible time (before changing into my favourite attire, being pyjamas). Most of the team would have preferred an official photo in rugby shorts and training singlet, but this was our inaugural entry into a game that had "not so much" encouraged female participation for too many years. We happily conformed, and besides, the fear of Joan Forno was real.

Thirty years on, the drought in Australia has finally broken. In your hands lies the first ever unofficial published Wallaroo history, specifically of the women's national team including the early games and tournaments. Aussies are familiar with both drought and flood but for some unknown reason, there has been a lack of history documented, archived, and reported about the women's game. It is super important for me to be able to pass on our history to the younger generations of Aussies and players worldwide, who probably don't even know the names of the pioneers nor the deep respect and love we original players have for certain people who deserve recognition.

I am hoping other Wallaroos, or the Australian Rugby Union (ARU) might even follow my lead and continue to document more of our women's rugby story. I can only report on the period in which I played. It would be great to get a full history of all the true pioneers, especially those who played in the early 1900s but were unsuccessful in maintaining a competition. We thank those un-named ladies and players who, for now, remain unknown. Please refer to my website (address to be added) and see if you can assist me in naming any of the un-named women photographed somewhere in Sydney in 1930 (part of the Sam Hood collection).

This book includes various parts of my life's journey. Rugby came in and out of my young adult years, so I needed to document the journey as it unfolded and chronologically (which I am hoping makes it easy and clear for the reader to follow). I am not a writer, but I have done my best to compile this record. Rugby occupied a significant chunk of my adult life and I will always be a fan and spectator of the game. I was a team member in the early 1990s until my 2nd World Cup appearance for Australia in Spain, 2002, where I played my final games of rugby at this level.

My "footy" journey commenced in Canberra, the capital city of our nation. As a result, stories and player histories from NSW, Queensland, and other states, will be totally different to mine. Some Australian states would take years to find enough interest and the players required to eventually compete in the annual women's rugby tournaments. It would be wonderful to have at least one story recorded from every Australian state including the players, volunteers, and staff who helped us all get onto the paddocks and running with the ball. A shout out to Tasi Woodard (coach of the Queensland women's team during 1996 & 1997) for documenting these two years of Queensland women's rugby.

I love rugby, as you may have guessed. It's a great game and my entry into the rugby world was never due to a need to prove a thing. The only reason was the love of the game and the culture which, at the time, came with it.

My retirement from international rugby was 10 years after I first started. These 10 years were some of the best years of my life and where some of my best mates were found. Rugby in that decade of my life was my highest priority. It is a privilege to retain a baggy green cap in my collection with the Australian coat of arms, the words Australian Rugby and my Wallaroo identity, #19. I was recently (June 2024) also capped in the state of NSW with a Waratahs baggy blue cap #100. Thanks to NSW Rugby, on the anniversary of 150 years, for recognising the female state players and inviting us into what used to be "the boys club". We now have females inducted into the NSW Rugby Hall of Fame as well as the Alumni. Massive thanks also go to Vanessa Bradley (Wallaroo #40) for the voluntary work and commitment she invested into the research of years' worth of records to enable this capping to occur.

It was during this rugby era from 1992 onwards, that women were finally permitted access to the game. It wasn't easy but we finally received the backing of the ARU, the support of the Australian public, the press and even our families (some of whom still believe that the female body was not designed nor created to play contact sport). I acknowledge that everyone is entitled to their own opinions. I thank God for free will and a society which is changing.

ADMIT ONE

My congratulations firstly go out to every single Wallaroo and every single member of our coaching and voluntary teams and staff across the years, from towns all across our huge nation. Massive thanks go to the families and partners who supported the players, including my own. These humans put up with us, our injuries, the out-of-pocket expenses, the absences from home and family responsibilities including the care of our children, meals, changes in lifestyle and relocation to access competition, training facilities, coaching and player resources and the endless request for assistance with fundraising. Thank you, we could not have achieved what we did without your love and support nor the financial sacrifices.

To the amazing volunteer coaches, the training staff, team management of all varieties, including team managers and medical volunteers, the referees, supporters, sponsors, promoters, members of the media and everyone else who believed that this dream of women playing rugby in Australia might come true. It bloody well did! Looking back, 30 years later, I feel proud. I still must pinch myself when I pass by a TV with a women's game being televised or while present in a grandstand at a live women's game. Is this really happening? Some days it still feels surreal.

The reality of what has been achieved by Australian women in rugby in the past 30 years is amazing. Massive congratulations to all who assisted in making this happen, especially to the Australian Rugby Union! I personally am grateful. There were so many hurdles that we had to overcome, many of which persist to this day. This year, being 2024, in Australia (my opinion and experience only), we continue to live in a patriarchy. This is the way it has always been since our British visitors arrived at Port Phillip Bay in 1788 and no doubt, the way it may continue to sadly be for a while longer (possibly until the Wallaroos sort out the situation up at Parliament House!).

Prior to the privilege of playing in that first international in Sydney, I was a member of the first Australian Women's Rugby Union Development Squad of 1993. This team was selected from the 1992 tournament in Newcastle, NSW. These were the days when there first existed hope that our Australian women might one day be good enough to enter the international women's rugby union arena. These were also the days when our "national kit" was embroidered with the "Wallabies" logo or "Australian Rugby", rather than an identity of our own.

The initial plan to send an Aussie team to the 1994 Women's Rugby World Cup would be taken away soon after our development squad was announced (1993). We were told we might be preparing for an international Test Match but not a World Cup appearance, because apparently, we weren't yet good enough for the ARU (sadly we didn't have the experience nor knowledge of the game required as there had been no competition for us to participate in). How the ARU expected us to improve is beyond me but thank God for us Canberrans, we still had a weekend rugby league competition to play and enjoy. The Wallaroos would have to learn the fine art of waiting.

Wallaroo #19 refers to the number on the back of my first ever Australian jersey (a reserve forward). It is also the same number of the baggy green cap which would be presented to me 14 years after my first international appearance. Like I said, there was lots of waiting in the women's game. I honestly do feel honoured to have been presented with my cap.

The logo embroidered on the left breast of my first green and gold jersey looked very different to the modern-day version. The colour of the jersey was a deep gold, like that of a stunning sunrise in Australia.

Glued into one of my scrap books is a small piece of gold paper with the typed words: "Australian Wallaroos 1994, may this pin be a memento and reminder of your first selection and the 'good times' in the FIRST AUSTRALIAN WOMEN'S RUGBY TEAM". This small token along with the pin, remains among the most precious items of my memorabilia. It also reminds me of the personal and beautiful touch of our president, manager, coach and extraordinary supporter of women's rugby, Mrs Joan Forno.

Even though I broke my nose at least six times during my rugby union playing career, suffered endless knocks to the head and every single

ADMIT ONE

part of my body, I still have the memories of these wonderful years of my life. Before dementia and aging kicks in, I have combed through the handwritten diaries which I wrote and have retained. I stored documents from every tournament and overseas trip whilst playing for Australia and the various states and clubs which I represented. These are treasured memories.

My scrap books contain media clippings from the first mention of my name in the women's rugby league team (1991) and every single official and unofficial communication that was sent to me. I am one of those humans who like to keep important things (to me anyway). These include my initial involvement in women's rugby league and rugby union as well as the women's sevens game.

My rugby treasure chest contains memorabilia saved from this amazing period of my life. This includes various playing and swapped jerseys (minus the ones which I have donated to various clubs or gifted to special friends), various playing shorts and socks from countries all around the world, my number ones (the formal kit including the blazers and scarves), trophies, trinkets, programs, table cards, event tickets and invitations, a box of VHS recordings and so many other memories.

Just to relieve some players' minds before I get into the next chapter, rest assured Wallaroos and other teammates, nothing illegal, immoral, or unsavoury has been reported within the pages of this book. Those stories are for oral opportunities for Wallaroos only (and to ensure that my four young sons are not privy to the antics that I got up to during my playing and partying career)! What goes on tour stays on tour, so it is said.

The following pages will give you an insight into how the game of women's rugby league, women's rugby union and women's rugby sevens team got started in Canberra, Australia. I discovered that I could not possibly write a book solely about the women's rugby union journey without including my personal involvement with the game of women's rugby league (which preceded union in the absence of a competition).

Note: so many of our amazing players of Australian rugby union came from other sporting codes, like netball, basketball, touch football, oztag, athletics, soccer, etc. Without my experience and years spent in the amazing game that women's rugby league brought to my life, I may have never discovered nor even played women's rugby union. Although this is not the case for every women's rugby union representative, it is my story and I believe significant as this book will cover more than just the history of women's sport in our country. I am hoping I can share a little bit of Aussie culture too and my life outside and inside of these various sports too.

My aim throughout these pages, is to take you back to 1991 where my rugby league journey started in the East Canberra Women's Team. Following on, in chronological order, I will take you to Newcastle, NSW (1992) where the Inaugural Women's Challenge, Rugby Union was played and share with you details of the subsequent annual tournaments during my era.

My playing history and this reflection expands into the journey of international women's rugby 7s and our arrival in Hong Kong (1997) as a team called "Aussie Gold".

I have included details of Australia's first appearance at an International Women's World Cup, as my journey took me not only into that adventure in Amsterdam, Holland (1998) but also to where I played my final game, Barcelona, Spain during Australia's second performance in the international 15s arena where I retired from playing women's rugby union.

But first, I wanted to share with you a little bit of rugby history: The first records of any female worldwide playing rugby union have been traced back to the handwritten diary of a girl called Emily Valentine. This isn't to say that another female hadn't played somewhere else in the world, only that a record of a female playing rugby was discovered.

The year was 1887, the country was Ireland and the reason for her involvement was that her brothers' team was short of players. Emily was apparently slotted into the backline so that the team could avoid a forfeit.

ADMIT ONE

More than one of her brothers played in that same team during that same game. History was made. Emily scored a try in that game on that day. God bless the Irish! What a day for the Valentine family. Emily's diary was found after her death and the writings clearly retell that first and subsequent games. These writings are the oldest and first record of any female playing the game of rugby worldwide (thus far).

The Wallaroos were not only 107 years behind the English in arriving on the paddock, but we were also approximately 12 years behind the "rest of the world" in the women's game. Unbeknown to most Australian women, the game was already being played by women internationally and worldwide.

You have now been admitted. Welcome to my history of women's rugby in Oz.

Note: a common Australian "thingy" or bad habit throughout our nation and lands, is to alter the "Queen's English" into "Australian", otherwise known as slang. If you are unsure about the meaning of a word, please refer to my glossary at the back of this book.

I hope you enjoy this trip down memory lane. I have enjoyed researching and compiling it. In the process I have contacted some good old rugby mates who I consider family, the chosen variety as opposed to biological. No matter how long in between contacts with old rugby mates, that bond remains strong as does the love we have for each other. This book and the timing of our 30-year anniversary seemed the perfect combination for me to leave another mark on women's sport in Australia. What a privilege.

International timeline of women's rugby union

1982 First ever international women's Test was played in the Netherlands during their 50-year anniversary celebrations, Utrecht. Netherlands vs France. France won 4-0.

1983 Women's Football Union was formed (England, Scotland and Wales)

1984 First ever National Women's Championships, USA (Chicago), eight teams

1987 First year that USA women played Canada (British Columbia), Canada

1987 First women's Test between Wales and England (Pontypool in Wales), England won 22-4

1988 First women's New Zealand team (Canterbury) left their country and participated on international circuit (eight-week tour including 21 games)

1989 New Zealand field first ever national women's team. A game against a touring US team from California was played.

1990 Rugby Fest, officially the "Women's World Rugby Festival", was a two-week festival of women's rugby, held in Christchurch, New Zealand late August - September

1991 First Women's Rugby World Cup, Wales. USA Winners.

1992 First ever Australian National Championships (Newcastle, NSW), four Australian teams

ADMIT ONE

1994 First international women's Test between Australia and New Zealand (North Sydney Oval, 2nd September)

1994 Second Women's Rugby World Cup, Scotland (after event was cancelled in the Netherlands)

1997 Inaugural Women's Rugby 7s Tournament, Hong Kong

1998 Third Women's Rugby World Cup, Barcelona (first time this tournament was sanctioned by the IRB). Wallaroos first appearance.

1999 First women's rugby union "Five Nations", later developed into the Six Nations (England, Ireland, Scotland, Wales, Italy and France)

1999 Second Women's Rugby 7s Tournament, Hong Kong

2002 Fourth Women's Rugby World Cup, Spain

2016 Women's rugby 7s played at Olympics for first time (Rio)

2019 England Women's Rugby Team offered full time contracts making them first team worldwide to be fully professional

2

WARM UP

Prior to taking you into the official "warm-up" of the history of women playing rugby in Australia, I thought it might be useful for you to understand a bit about me. I enjoyed two full decades of living prior to me discovering this game.

Whilst working and living in the Northern Territory for more than 10 years and working as a remote police officer for most of this time, I would personally meet, get to know, and love, hundreds of First Nations people. Men, women and children, born in the bush and raised there. I lived alongside these tribes in various communities, including but not limited to Warlpiri, Pintubi, Alyawarra, Kaytetye and Warumungu people. I sat in the red dirt and listened to their stories.

These people taught me a lot. Some of them I consider family, especially the ones who named and called me Nunngarryi. The ladies taught me how to hunt in their traditional ways, digging for ants and bush potato, finding honey and bush raisins and so much more. The men taught me how to gut and cook a kangaroo on the fire, shoot bush turkey and took me to places that many "white fellas" have not visited. I ate witchetty grubs, budgerigar, emu, camel, and most of the bush foods cooked for me (but never the intestines)!

I witnessed their tracking skills, listened to their prayer and stories that have been handed down for thousands of years, I watched them create dot paintings, play some amazing sport and much more whilst living in these desert areas. I learned new languages and words to describe things in their culture that were very different to mine. I tried hard to reason with their law when it clashed with that of the NT police and "white fella". I participated in a lifestyle closely connected to the oldest known humans worldwide. That was a privilege and the memories and friendships made are long lasting.

I shared cups of billy tea and ate kangaroo tail cooked on an open fire while listening to members of the Warlpiri tribe, present during and survivors of the Coniston Massacre (August 1928) share the stories. During these occasions, I felt not only sad but ashamed to wear the NT police uniform. This uniform represented police officers who killed innocent First Nations people during those four days of that massacre just outside of Yuendumu (a remote community that I called home from 2002 – 2003). This massacre was only one of hundreds that occurred in our history of Australia. To say it was "close to home", is an understatement. I don't have the words to describe how disgraceful and tragic some of our Australian history really is. I am sorry for what happened.

I personally wish to acknowledge the traditional custodians of this nation. I shout out and thank the Ngunnawal tribe (southern NSW and ACT) where I am sitting to type my words for this book and the land where I was raised. I respectfully choose to acknowledge the connection to land, water and spirit of all First Nations people of our country. I pay my personal respects to elders past, present and emerging and I pray to God that one day, peace and serenity will be discovered. I wish we could change our past, sadly I can only learn from the mistakes that have been made (and my own too)! I am teaching my own children the truth and believe that all Australians have a part to play towards reconciliation.

WARM UP

I thought it might also be useful for you to get to know me personally before stepping into the story of my footy journey. This might help you to understand how I even became an international women's rugby union player (both 15s and 7s), selected as a dual representative in both codes of women's footy (league and union) and how the hell I got dragged along to my very first game in June 1991.

I was born on Melbourne Cup Day, 2nd of November, 1971, in a hospital in Newcastle, New South Wales. A New Zealand-bred horse called Silver Knight was brought "across the ditch" to race that same day. That bugger of a thoroughbred beat me to the finish line. Silver Knight and jockey crossed in first place and ever since then, I have been trying to outdo those bloody Kiwis without much luck. I arrived at this world with a competitive streak and a love for winning (which isn't just limited to sport)!

In the liturgical calendar, this date that I was born is also known as the Feast of All Souls or Holy Souls. I consider myself blessed to have grown up in this "lucky country". I lived the life afforded to most Aussie kids, born during this era of our nation's history. I flourished in the sunshine, our amazing weather, and the outdoors where clean drinking water is readily available, and life is relatively safe.

I spent the first week of my life in a hospital with my mum, Patricia Irene Andrew (nee Curtis). Mum hails from Ganmain, a small country town in the Riverina of NSW outside of a town called Wagga Wagga. My dad is John Wallace Andrew of East Melbourne. Dad was at home in Newcastle, possibly wearing Mum's apron and runners, during that first week in November 1971, wrangling my five older siblings. The baby Margaret (who had just been knocked off the perch as being the youngest of the tribe), had not yet even celebrated her first birthday.

At least I had won something that day (bloody Silver Knight)! I was crowned the baby of our family and held this position for just over two years before Catherine arrived. This period was long enough for me to learn some of the survival skills required to survive my childhood.

WALLAROO #19

Like most Aussie kids, we spent a lot of time outdoors. Fortunately for me, when my neighbourhood mates were busy, I had family. My older brothers all played various sports and when I was too young to play or even fill in, we spectated or found mischief in the nearby playing fields. Separate to that, I would be riding my bike in the pine forest up the road from our family home, visiting the local shops and playing at the nearby park and bushland.

My sporting career first took shape in the backyard of our family home at 18 Renmark Street. Dad's work had seen the family relocated from Newcastle to Canberra and by the time we settled in, I was on the move from walking to running, and fast. If you didn't have speed to get to the plate of food on the table, you simply missed out. It was a matter of survival of the fittest in my family. I was a terribly fussy eater as a kid. Mum never forced me to eat anything I didn't want to eat. I ate a lot of cornflakes with milk for dinner if I turned my nose up at my mum's cooking and lamb's fry. I preferred plain food to spicy or saucy as a kid and I have a love of vegemite like most Aussie kids (especially on the crust).

I'd play hopscotch for hours on end with my sisters on the cement driveway which Dad painted for us, engaged in skipping games with ropes, doing handstands and entering competitions as to whom could suspend their body in the air for the longest period of time. I loved jumping on the trampoline (after waiting for my turn in the family queue, which could take hours), climbing trees in the backyard, shooting goals, playing handball and endless hours of cricket and basketball.

My dad had hand built a BBQ from bricks in our backyard. This beauty would later serve as a solid platform for jumping off, using it to lever myself over the fence to retrieve countless balls that were kicked or thrown over the back fence or to take a short cut to a mate's home. There is no doubt, I first learned the art of catching and passing from my siblings in the backyard. I had to work hard for my skills. My genetics, from both sides of my family tree, set me up well for a solid, strong, well-balanced, and healthy body. I have been blessed with good health for the majority of my life thus far.

WARM UP

At the top of Renmark Street lies the Mount Stromlo Pine Forest. It is a bloody challenging bike ride from number 18 to the very top of the street, yet from my earliest memories I would challenge myself to ride all the way to the top without getting off my bike or stopping and giving up. I was one of those kids who always skipped over the crack in the concrete footpath in case it brought me bad luck. I would challenge myself at every opportunity (like racing myself up the 20 steps from the driveway to the front door in Olympic record time, every single time)!

The "pineos" provided kilometres of dirt trails, endless rows of pine and eucalyptus trees, a dam (with yabbies caught using a hand line and net), kangaroos, cattle, birds, spiders, and insects of all kinds and loads of places to explore. I loved the forest and still do. The thought of even the scent of those pine trees takes me back to some wonderful childhood memories and wide-open spaces that I was free to explore.

My primary schooling was fun. It was filled to the brim with great times and good friends. I was educated by the sisters of the Holy Family of Nazareth. These catholic nuns were major players in my childhood; they were teachers, singers, sports coaches, and highly capable women dressed in traditional habit and a veil. These nuns played hard, were highly competitive and played to win. I am guessing this is where I first was exposed to fierce competition (my mum didn't have a spare five minutes for herself nor to enjoy any sports aside from spectating) so I am sure it was these nuns who inspired me in many ways in sport. The nuns would have us marching along to band music on the outdoor bitumen areas before the school bell rang and even in the freezing cold months of a Canberra winter. We even had morning exercise in the school hall (the health hustle). Music was played, similar to an aerobics class, except the instructor was a catholic nun dressed in a veil wearing runners and pushing us physically to our limits.

Netball became my childhood sport, which was typical for young girls in the early 1980s in Australia. Mum had registered me aged 7 years for the St. Jude's Lollypops Team. We were coached under the guidance of a holy nun, Sr. Irene Maree Rodak (who taught me in school when I was aged 7 and 9 and was my all-time favourite nun and teacher). Sr Irene Maree was quietly competitive and a great netball player too. Sister was a great coach, highly accurate shooter of goals with the netball, umpire and an all-round amazing human being whom I love dearly. Sister coached our Lollypops team for six consecutive years. We played every Saturday morning during the winter competition in rain, hail, fog, frost, and sunshine.

During my teenage years, I switched across from playing "C" in netball to "point guard" in basketball. There were no such thing as mixed teams back then, it was all girls. Each year of my education from about 8 years of age right through until 18 years, I represented my school in athletics (sprints both short and longer distances up to 1500 metres), cross country and various other team sports. I loved the challenge and competition that sport brought to my head and heart. I also loved being outside, which is where most sports were played in my day.

My secondary education was spent at St Clare's College, Griffith ACT. The school was one of the largest catholic all girls' schools in Canberra. I wasn't given a choice to attend there, I simply did what my parents told me to and followed my older sisters along to the bus stop out the front of our home. I enjoyed my time at St Clare's and was guided by some amazing men and women. The school motto is "Seek Wisdom", something which I continue to practice in greater depth these days. I am a work in progress.

Growing up in a large family set me up well to participate in various teams, not only in sports but later in a range of employment opportunities. I also developed numerous positive and negative attributes from childhood. These qualities went hand in hand with the teams in which I worked and played. I developed into a typical adult child with a range of skills but lacked many that are required to live a balanced and healthy life. I am working on unlearning and learning a wide range of skills, these days in recovery.

WARM UP

After graduating from Year 12 I embarked on my first overseas trip to the UK at the age of 18 years with my good mate Kylie. I travelled throughout the British Isles, Europe and Canada. I didn't play any type of organised sport for this entire year, but I certainly accumulated some miles on my brand-new pushy which I bought in a bike shop in Oxford.

Kylie and I lived and worked in a catholic boarding school called Rye St Antony's in Headington Hill. I worked with the primary school-aged children, while Kylie was in another boarding house with the teenagers. I loved the job, my role and the children. That push bike was the first one I paid for out of my own adult pay check and in English pounds. It was a white-coloured 5-speed women's racer, something I would never buy again yet rode so proudly amongst the thousands of bike riders and students of Oxford. That pushy and I travelled the British Isles (without any helmet)! I have always loved riding and still do.

The original plan for me, after spending that period abroad, was to attend university and complete a degree. But when I returned to Australia, I had caught some form of travel bug and furthering my education was not at the top of my priority list.

It was during my first year at university that I became involved in women's rugby league. I played from 1991 until 1994 and was fortunate enough to travel widely within Australia and across the ditch to New Zealand for my very first playing tour of any sport (1992). A rugby league tournament for women was held in Auckland, and our Canberra team was the only team registered from outside NZ. That was an amazing experience as well as an introduction to the absolute beauty that New Zealand offers.

WALLAROO #19

My parents and I (1991)

I love New Zealand, and I hate to be beaten by them (and their horses)! There is no doubt about it, the Kiwi comes from one of the most stunning countries worldwide. They are also, without a doubt, gifted and talented athletes, and always proved very hard to beat. It is only my opinion and experience but from what I learned and witnessed, New Zealanders live and breathe rugby from a very early age. Rugby seems to be the major sport and played by the majority of Kiwis, therefore encouraged by the parents and siblings of families, in contrast to here in Oz where we play a wider variety of sports.

After my initiation to women's rugby union in 1992, I had the pleasure of playing for and travelling within various Australian states including my original home state ACT, New South Wales, South Australia, Queensland, Western Australia, and the Northern Territory. I played both footy codes for several years.

I went on to play for Australia at two international women's rugby union World Cup tournaments in Holland (1998) and Spain (2002). I also had the absolute privilege of representing Australia (Aussie Gold) four times over at the Hong Kong Women's Sevens Tournament in 1997, 1999, 2000 and finally in 2001.

By the age of 31 years, I was ready to say goodbye to competitive rugby and pass my boots on to someone else that I knew would appreciate the opportunity. It was a lot of rugby, a lot of travel and so much fun. I walked away from rugby by choice and while I was still able to walk (without ever suffering any major breaks nor serious injury) after all those wonderful years. I was satisfied and looking forward to the next major challenge which would replace rugby.

3

LEAGUE CAME FIRST

In Sydney, during the year 1921, two brave women wrote to the NSW rugby league seeking permission to start up a women's rugby league competition. These legends were Molly Cane and Nellie Doherty, a pair of young women from North Sydney.

Molly and Nellie loved watching the men play rugby league and desperately wanted to play too. They were aware that women were playing soccer in England and France in the 1900s and they felt that rugby league for women in Oz would follow a similar trajectory.

On the 26th of May that year, the girls received the green light to proceed with their proposal. Meetings were held and like most groups of women, regardless of the era or sporting code, a committee was elected. The voted president was Molly Cane.

A referee called Miller attended the very first training run along with two police officers to ensure that the men stayed clear of the training and there were no issues. Women needed to learn the laws of the game, practice how to tackle, kick and generally improve fitness. At this historic gathering, approximately 100 females of all ages joined in. Every Friday afternoon, for the next three months, the ladies would repeat the same. There were no reported problems.

Finally, game day arrived, and the very first recorded women's rugby league match took place in Australia. The game was played at Moore Park, Sydney. The date was Saturday, 17th of September, 1921. The two teams were Metropolitan (Metro) in a blue coloured jersey, and Sydney who wore maroon. There were no other games played prior to nor after this match (aside from the women's footrace). It was purely an exhibition of women's rugby league, 1921 style.

These legendary pioneers of the women's game were:

Metro Blues: M.Neilson; Maggie Maloney, Nellie Doherty (Captain), D.Gray, H.Allenby; E.Gillet, A.Mathenius; S.Williams, S.Mack, Eulalie Stagpoole, G.McCann, L.Gillet, J.Burton.

Sydney Reds: C.Beckett; L.Lewan, D.Ling, M.Hunt, K.Skehan; M.McGarry, G.Hoskins (c); M.Chubb, B.Beavan, L.Farman, D.Johns, A.Alderson, M.Phelps.

Referee: Mr Ted Kerr.

A crowd of about 20,000 were present in Sydney to witness this historic game. Metro won it 21-11, but the scoreline was irrelevant. This game was historic for women in Australia. Congratulations to these pioneers of women's rugby league.

70 years on from that historic match at Moore Park, the great game of rugby league for women was re-activated.

Without any knowledge of the history of Molly and Nellie, nor the next "movement" of the women's game in the 1950s and again in the 1980s, another Sydney woman would reignite the game for women in the nation's capital city, Canberra.

LEAGUE CAME FIRST

Fiona Buchanan was a 19-year-old rugby league supporter. She had tired of watching her brother have all the fun on the paddock and set off to do something about it.

After moving from Sydney to Canberra, Fiona met with Canberra Raiders player Steve Walters and discussed with him her urge to play. Steve agreed to help. Planning was instantly undertaken and, just like Molly and Nellie 70 years earlier, a women's committee was formed. The Canberra Raiders Club had offered some financial assistance, which will always be greatly appreciated.

This hard-working women's rugby league committee of 1991 included: President: Carole Simkins, Secretary: Katrina Bush, Treasurer: Merrilyn Kemp, Registrar: Glenda Merritt, Additional members: Janita Mannie, Liz Elliot, Marissa Huettner, Penny Brown and Tracey Wilson. Publicity officer was Sue Fenely.

It was Taylor Park in Queanbeyan, NSW, which hosted the inaugural gathering of women from Canberra and Queanbeyan (NSW). Fiona and Steve were present to greet the women who responded to a newspaper ad seeking players.

These pioneers in Canberra included: Karen McQualter, Penny Brown, Marissa Huettner, Leanne Cosgrove (Williams), Sue Feneley, Cath Welch, Glenda Merritt, Jenny Duffy and Janita Mannie. A shout goes out to my mate, Cath Welch, a legend of the women's rugby league game and lifetime member who was present from the very beginning. Cath trusted me with her own treasure chest of personal records, scrap books and photo albums from the good old days.

Brett Kelly and John Stanley (Canberra Raiders players) joined Steve Walters and assisted in coaching the girls along with Brian Bourke (ACT and Royals rugby union) as trainer. Steve Walters gained more support from the Canberra Raiders Club who provided the training paddock and lights, playing jerseys and training equipment. Momentum and interest in the sport was growing.

Soon enough, there were enough girls to form two teams of seven players per side. Young girls and adults appeared from all corners of the ACT and Queanbeyan. These included high school students as young as 14 years old (who required parental permission to train and play), public servants, teachers, nurses, university students and mothers.

Steve was the first coach of the squad of Canberra combined with New South Wales women's players, and he was also present to watch the very first match. Note: the NSW town of Queanbeyan is located about 20km from Canberra which is located in the Australian Capital Territory (ACT). Therefore, this historic match would be a combination of both states given that players from this first squad were a combination of the two (and the fact that these two towns are physically located so close together).

The 13th of March, 1991, arrived, exactly 69 years, 9 months and 2 weeks after the very first women's "exhibition game" in Sydney, 1921 (Note: previous attempts to have a rugby league competition for women in Canberra had been trialled in an earlier decade but didn't last). This game was played in between the men's matches of the John Braddon Management A-grade Challenge Cup and the Schweppes U19 knockout. This game and the others that followed were played as the "curtain raisers" during the pre-season period in Canberra and under lights. This historic first game was played with only seven players per side on a full-sized field and for 15 minutes.

The second match in this seven-per-side competition was also staged at West Belconnen on the following Wednesday night. The Cougars played against the Jaguars. The quality of play had improved even from the first game, the girls were loving the challenge and experience, and the spectators were entertained by the girls on the field.

The follow-on from this pre-season 7s experience and its success led to the development of a four-team premiership competition which was played on a weekly basis in Canberra (on Saturdays during daylight hours). The improvement seen from the first pre-season game to the first local competition game was noticeable. The players gained knowledge and confidence, while passing and tackling skills improved quickly. The women's game was on the improve and more advertising continued, along with the word-of-mouth whispers. Players such as Sue Fenley, Carole Simkins, Cath Welch and others dragged players out from all walks of life and locations. Thank you, ladies, for your persistence, enthusiasm, and service to the game both on and off the field.

The four women's teams who registered for the first ever nine-per-side competition in 1991 were affiliated with a variety of local Canberra rugby league clubs, these being Woden Valley Rams, West Belconnen, Gunghalin Gallopers and East Canberra. The scrums were made up of only three women per side and games were played on the full-size field under international rules. The halves were 20 minutes each and games were played prior to the local first grade men's fixtures. This stage of the development of the game is where I would wander onto the field for the first time.

This local competition in Canberra grew stronger and larger with each week. Unbeknownst to me during these early months of 1991, history for women's sport was being made and in my hometown. During these months while the girls were busy getting fit and gaining experience in the game, I was settling back into a life in Canberra after my year abroad. I was trying to concentrate on my studies, but I was busy dreaming of my next overseas adventure.

My personal history with the game of women's rugby league started out by chance through a friend. This champion human is Helen Wylks, originally of Holder (and the same parish of St Jude's). Helen was a part of the pre-season seven-per-side hit competition. She was enthusiastic about the new sport and was very keen to convince me to come along and try it out. I wasn't quite so keen. I would see Helen coming towards me in the university halls and hide. I constantly made excuses for why I preferred not to come along and give this new sport a go. Nothing about the game grabbed my interest – until that very first game when my life changed.

My rugby league journey began one sunny Saturday morning during June 1991. Helen appeared, standing at the front door of our family home in

Duffy. She stood dressed in her playing gear, her car parked in the driveway with the engine still running, begging me to join her as the team were short and needed a few extra players. I agreed.

Upon arriving at the sports ground in Belconnen, I could hear this stern, loud, female Kiwi voice, barking orders and instructing the team during the warm-up. Helen and I had arrived late, and I sensed this familiar feeling inside of me, that I might be in trouble for something that potentially had nothing to do with me. I felt terrified. That Kiwi voice was the captain/coach, a brilliant player by the name of Louise Ferris (also known as Ferrit).

At this stage I wondered why the heck I had got into that vehicle with Helen. I must have been insane. My nerves hit me right in the gut and I wanted to run in the opposite direction as fast as I could. Helen's huge smile and comforting words got me closer to the playing field. The two of us undertook a very short warm up before running onto the paddock to play. The rest, as they say, is history.

Prior to taking the field that day, my experience with rugby league amounted to casually walking past my mother, in her element, on Friday nights in our family home spectating (at that stage I had no clue there were two rugby codes). Mum could be heard yelling at Ricky Stuart and Laurie Daley on the tele from her armchair. She is a long and loyal Canberra Raiders supporter. I am pretty sure the neighbourhood all went out on Friday nights to avoid hearing my mother yelling at the TV screen. Mum already had priors for yelling at her seven children, especially on weekday mornings as she attempted to get us all out the front door to school.

We had three televisions in our family home. One was located in the playroom, another sat on a wheelable trolley in the kitchen, and the third, the one with the largest screen, sat in the loungeroom, the most comfortable room in the house with carpet flooring and an old-style oil heater.

On a Friday night during footy season, Mum would have all three TVs going at the same time! The volume on the tele was high and there was a different game or program shown on each screen, and at the same

LEAGUE CAME FIRST

time, Mum was tuned into her trusty transistor radio (a wireless). She preferred the ABC football commentary as opposed to the channel nine commentators on the tele, so the main TV was muted and the tranny was blaring on full volume while she knitted and watched and constantly checked the different screens. I am talking every Friday night during the footy season and every possible television! My dad was nowhere to be found and usually smoking his Benson and Hedges cigarettes on the back veranda enjoying a cold beer and the peace and quiet.

My lack of knowledge of the game of rugby league and the rules were further proved during that very first game I played at Belconnen. I got a touch of the ball at some stage during the first half. I was out on the left wing alone, I think Helen had passed me the ball and I just naturally tucked it tightly underneath my left armpit and "ran like buggery". The only way I knew how to run was via the quickest route and that appeared to be in a straight line and straight for those goal posts.

I really had no idea what to do with the ball once I had got past the opposition and was standing alone on the other side of the try line. I decided to gently drop the ball over the line and head back to my team. I was clueless, I had no idea I had lost the ball for my team during that process of "not scoring" my very first try. I had a lot to learn and did manage to ground the ball over the try line after Loui explained a few rules to me during the half time break.

From that Saturday onwards, I never missed a training session nor a game if I could help it. I was hooked, instantly. My mates in the East Canberra Team were a group of legends. I was surrounded by some real talent, and I soon cottoned on to the laws and how to play this great game. The team were keen to improve, in fitness, skills and laws, and it was infectious.

Given there were only four teams in our local competition, most of us knew each other by the end of the season. Training was fun, I loved the physical nature of it and the challenges of racing, fitness and competing against my teammates.

WALLAROO #19

The 1991 East Canberra team included: Anna Willcock, Helen Wylks, Carole Simpkins, Katrina Maddon, Darlene Riley, Kylie Baker, Glenda Merritt, Louise Ferris, Megan Mitchell, Carolyn Walsh and I. Louise was our captain and usually the coach until someone brave enough to take us on appeared on the scene.

During June 1991, my first month of playing this new game, there was an opportunity for me to play representative footy. I grabbed this experience with both hands. Two teams represented the ACT at the Illawarra knockout which comprised eight teams, with the East Canberra combined team winning.

In July, the following month, I would have my first taste of a big game. A women's representative team from Sydney had been invited to play in a Canberra game, but this team withdrew about two weeks before kick-off. Organisers of the local rugby league competition decided we would split the Canberra playing base (which was about 60 women) and we would put on an exhibition match to show off the local talent. This would be the first time many locals saw women playing rugby league during this era.

1st game of women's rugby league played
at Bruce Stadium, ACT (1991)

LEAGUE CAME FIRST

This game made history. We were well supported by the home crowd which included our own families and friends. The game was played during half-time of the Canberra Raiders vs Brisbane Broncos reserve grade match at Bruce Stadium (now called GIO Stadium). This was the first time, in the history of the men's Winfield Cup Competition, that women's rugby league was included during a round game. It wasn't just an honour to be on the field that day, it was great fun.

Our East Canberra Women's Team played and won the Grand Final at Seiffert Oval on Saturday 14th September 1991 against the Gunghalin Gallopers Women's Team. I had joined a team of quality players who became close friends on and off the field.

On this same day, an ACT women's team (chosen from the two teams not in the Grand Final) travelled to Wagga Wagga, NSW to play against a representative team from the Illawarra. This game was played with 13 per side with interchange rules for 60 minutes. Illawarra were far stronger than our Canberra side and ran out winners 22-4. Looking back there were women from these early league days who also popped up in rugby union teams in different states in future years. I guess some of us who played women's rugby league, followed the same trajectory.

The Canberra Women's Rugby League were instrumental in getting the nation organised; we had such an enthusiastic playing base and group of volunteers. In October 1991, we held a round robin tournament in Queanbeyan which was attended by teams from Sydney, Illawarra, Canberra and South Australia. East Canberra won that tournament with another local team, the Rams, finishing third. Annual women's tournaments were up and going with teams from other states also wanting to join in and compete in this great game – the game which is today played in every state of Australia. The same game, this year in 2024, which sold out an entire stadium of fans at the Women's State of Origin Clash in Newcastle, NSW.

Other early legends of the women's game who were instrumental from the beginning were coaches: Graham Willard (who went on to become the first Australian women's coach in the history of our game) and John Squizzy Taylor, a talented sports trainer and coach and supporter of our game. Although every team indeed had a coach (or sometimes a player like Ferrit), Graham and Squizzy stood out and stayed around for years to come. Thanks gents! Not only for the footy but for the amazing times we shared and the fun we had.

Early in 1992 saw the selection of players for an ACT team to tour New Zealand. Training began in late January accompanied by heaps of fundraising efforts by the players. Our team took part in a 10-day tour of the North Island, NZ. We arrived in Auckland on the Easter Weekend of 1992 for the one-day tournament on Easter Sunday.

Our team comprised of: Libby Andrew, Leanne Cosgrove, Alison Cox, Louise Ferris, Karen Hendrick, Marissa Huettner, Bronwyn Johnston, Katrina Madden, Glenda Merritt, Darlene Riley, Carole Simpkins, Alison Smith, Cath Welch, Vanessa Willard, Anna Willock, Tracey Wilson and Helen Wylks. Coaching and management staff were: G. Brewer, P. Kaden, J. Taylor (coach).

The day was huge, we played game after game in perfect conditions but sadly lost the Grand Final in the last minute of extra time! Those bloody Kiwis sure knew how to spoil our fun. I am pretty sure we evened up the results after winning the boat races (otherwise known as drinking games) in the bar later that evening. We had finally gained a taste of rugby league and the standard in the North Island of NZ around this time. We were competitive and brought across a strong side from Canberra.

This tournament was the first time that Aussie women would play rugby league across the ditch in New Zealand. We were kicking goals and scoring tries and having some great fun. We made new friends and memories everywhere we went.

Our tour headed on to the Waitomo Cave, while we also enjoyed a visit to Rotorua and the hot springs. There were more parties, the first and only bungee jump of my life, white water rafting, a terrifying jet boating experience and many other pleasures of this amazing first international tour of my playing history. Home was calling and on the 10th day we returned to Canberra via Sydney, exhausted and broke but not broken. My love of this game had grown, and my enthusiasm was on the rise too.

The local Canberra women's competition of 1992 had four teams registered; sadly, the team from Gunghalin folded, but were replaced by a new team from the Tuggeranong Valley called the "Buffalos". The Woden Valley Rams, East Canberra and West Belconnen Women's Teams all returned for the second year of the local women's rugby league competition. Our East Canberra Rugby League Women's Team were undefeated this whole 1992 local season. We won the Grand Final at Seiffert Oval for the second year of my playing career on the 13th of September, 1992. Fun and competition were at a maximum level; I had really grasped this game and my position as hooker suited my skills and speed well.

A representative squad was again selected that year, and we played against the Illawarra women (Wollongong, NSW). On the 29th of August, 1992, we travelled via minibus to Wagga Wagga and were beaten again! Winning and losing rugby league games brought many experiences but the fun after the game and the antics post-match were equally as rewarding. ACT also played the North Sydney Women's Team in Sydney on the 26th of September, 1992.

On the October long weekend of 1992, a 10-per-side women's rugby league competition was held, in Canberra (10 – 11th October). Seven teams participated in this amazing competition at Rugby League Park, Braddon. East Canberra, my team, came away with the winner's trophy. It was an amazing weekend of footy and fun.

My rugby league journey went on and on. More and more games and learnings. When the next season arrived, I was back into pre-season training again and part of the same team.

When the June long weekend of 1993 came around, I was again a member of the Canberra Royal Wallaroos Women's Rugby Union Team, heading to Newcastle (on that same Royals Rugby bus) for the second women's rugby union competition. At the end of this event, a National Development Squad had been named. I made the team and felt excited.

By the end of the 1993 rugby league season, our East Canberra women's team had won another Grand Final, which we did on the 12th of September, 1993. We played this game at Seiffert Oval against the same opposition and enjoyed the same good fun and competition. I never tired of the games nor the familiarity. I loved every challenge, every training session, game and after-party. These were wonderful years of my life where some amazing achievements and memories were made.

My final tournament for the 1993 women's rugby league year was the Australian Club Championships at O'Connor Oval in North Canberra. Our East Canberra Women's Team, which had lost only one match in three years, scored 202 points in our seven matches of the championship without conceding one point. That final was played against Northern Districts (Illawarra) in the pouring rain. Our East Canberra team had six players named in the 10-player Australian Merit Team that weekend. I was one of these and one of the teammates bathed in glory and mud after diving and sliding in the muddy puddles following the final hooter. That weekend was one of my most memorable league championships of my career. When I reflect on the photos and the media article from that weekend, I am reminded of the amazing fun and friendships that were born out of these years of my life.

East Canberra Women's Winners (1993)

1994 arrived and I was still keen to play league. I registered for the same old team, yet this year we broke away from the East Canberra Club and formed a new team, called "Castaways".

Our team sponsor Pete Pomazak and his beloved wife Lannie came with us too. Lannie and Pete were amazing supporters of the women's game and there is no doubt in my mind that without the support and financial backing of these two amazing humans, we may never have got to the levels that we achieved in the record speed we did. We had the players with skill and commitment, but without financial backing, in the women's game, it was very difficult to achieve our dreams. So, to Pete and Lannie, THANK YOU. Your generosity, friendship, love and kindness will never be forgotten (even if you have left town to enjoy retirement).

My final year of playing women's rugby league was a really busy year filled with both codes of footy. The pre-season rugby league games kicked off in March/April with the new year season starting after the Easter Long Weekend.

Not only was I playing league on Saturdays this year, I was also in my first year of International Representative Rugby Union duties for the Australian Women's Rugby Union Squad. I played and trained for "footy" constantly. This was my life, and these were my choices.

By the end of the 1994 rugby league season, I had run in 132 points (33 tries). The next top three highest point scorers were: Penny Brown with 88, Louise Ferris with 84 and Vanessa Willard with 72. I loved playing rugby league and the feeling inside of me which came with the challenge of the training and games.

When mid-year arrived and it was time to register for the annual Newcastle road trip, I faced (along with the other teammates selected in that first developmental squad of 1993) an ultimatum from the Australian Rugby Union. Rob Bradley (ARU Development Officer) advised that we had to decide between league or union. We were no longer permitted to play both codes of footy. Although I was sad to have to wander away from the amazing game of league and the mates I left behind in that team and local competition, I was keen to explore this game called rugby union a little more.

To sign with the Australian Rugby Union, I paid the requested $5 to join the club. Leaving league and crossing over to union in 1994 was a decision I made without hesitation. I have no regrets.

During my absence from rugby league, the game would continue to develop, attracting more and more female players to the game. During this era of the game, the Canberra Women's Competition would continue to grow each and every year.

By the mid 1990s in Canberra, local competitions for women to play both codes (rugby league and rugby union) were available. Although in the infant stage, women were on the rugby paddocks and were improving with each game.

Rugby League Memories and Mates

NEWCASTLE, NSW

The first ever women's rugby union tournament in Australia was held in Newcastle in 1992. For three consecutive years, 1992, 1993 and 1994, women from all over Australia and elsewhere would return to Newcastle to play across the Queen's Birthday (June long weekend) annually. These tournaments were "round robin" arrangements played across two days and between club teams, as opposed to state or representative teams. It was early days for this new sport in Australia and it was great fun. I was a participant in those first three tournaments, playing for the Canberra Royals Wallaroo's Women's Team.

In 1995 and every year since then, an annual tournament for women's rugby has been played on a rotational basis, somewhere in Australia, never yet returning to Newcastle. The Australian Capital Territory (ACT) hosted the tournament in 1995, then Sydney in 1996 when for the very first time, state teams competed against state teams (as opposed to clubs teams playing other club teams and many from various states). This meant the competition by 1996 was growing and the standard of play was on the improve. Each state was only permitted to register one team. It was a great move for the sport and the development of the women's game.

This chapter will give you some idea of those first three years when Newcastle hosted the annual tournament and before women's rugby started to get serious in Australia. By 1995, it appeared that the game for women would not be closing shop again as it had in the past. It started to feel like this sport was finally here to stay and be taken a little more seriously than previous attempts to keep the game going.

1992

Before reaching the paddock

Kym Thurbon and Matt Brennan of the Royals Rugby Club, Canberra, responded to a request from the Australian Rugby Union. Their challenge was to attempt to find enough Canberra players to form a women's rugby team. Once these women were identified, the task was to get them organised to play in a rugby union tournament in Newcastle, NSW, located about 420 kilometres up the road. Not only had the girls never played before, but there was also no opposition to practice against. We had a borrowed set of old white Royals rugby club jerseys, three brave coaches, enough girls to field one team and a 21-seater bus to get us to Newcastle, as well as all the enthusiasm required to travel to Newcastle and win!

When I heard about the challenge and realised it would be held over a long weekend (meaning there was an extra day to travel and I would not be required to take leave from paid work), I was instantly interested. Along with the majority of our women's rugby league team (except two), I registered for the inaugural event. For whatever reason, I landed #7, the open side flankers' position, which has always been my favourite position in the code of rugby union. I would happily play any position if it meant being a part of the game on the field as opposed to warming the bench.

NEWCASTLE, NSW

In what felt like no time at all, I was sitting on the Royals Rugby Union bus amongst a bunch of familiar footy mates plus another ten odd new faces, bound for the town of my birth – Newcastle, NSW.

The long bus trips to and from rugby tournaments, from the very first experience to the very last one, over the years, were an extraordinarily fun and unexpected aspect of my rugby experience. Thinking about those days only makes me smile and giggle. Hours and hours were spent on the bus, not only getting to know each other but also discussing the game (pre and post), moves and what the hell we were supposed to do in this new game called rugby union. I had some idea about rugby league by this stage of my playing history, but I had never heard the words ruck and maul prior to that weekend. I was told the players in my "pack" were called "the forwards", otherwise known as "pigs". I was curious and went into the weekend with an open mind and high level of fitness and no experience whatsoever at the age of 20 years.

Over many years to come, that same core group of Canberra friends and teammates would undertake at least 30 more road trips to various rugby fields around New South Wales. The hours on the bus involved storytelling, singing, team meetings, dress-ups, recovery sessions, makeshift hospital wards (when travelling home to Canberra after being battered by opposing teams), an open bar, a changing room, a takeaway restaurant and so much more. A lot of our lives' problems, successes and challenges were discussed and shared in that enclosed space inside the safe walls of the Royals rugby bus. Players talked through issues, and we learned to trust and lean on each other. I honestly believe our Canberra side became such a strong force and good team because of this extra time spent together.

The back of the bus could be a dark and scary place to visit on some trips, but was also incredible fun. The seating was rotated and to any road user that was driving in the vicinity of our team bus in those days, on behalf of the team, I apologise for anything you may have witnessed or seen squished on the rear window. Frequent stops were made alongside the Hume and Federal Highways when returning home from a game. There were many emergency stops for the toilet, it must have been all that water we had consumed to avoid dehydration on the field (or a few too many beverages)! Ah, those were the good old days, before mobile phones and social media were invented.

Some of the trips were designated as "dress-ups", which meant that a theme would be decided and the whole team, including the coach and driver, participated. It was never compulsory, but it was heaps of fun if you joined in. Some of the themes were Saturday night '60s, a toga trip, frocks only, 1980s theme and a whole lot more (and less too). There is a rugby saying: "What goes on tour stays on tour" and I must adhere to the rugby laws and not tell the stories. I am not giggling at this point but laughing out loud at the memories and antics of my teammates. Thank you, ladies, for the great times and apologies to the teammates on the bus who may have been irritated by my actions, words, or behaviour during those younger days of my life. I apologise, especially to those girls trying to sleep or nursing an injury or concussion.

NEWCASTLE, NSW

Royals Rugby

WALLAROO #19

I am pretty sure that I had a turn sitting on every single seat of that Royals bus over the years. From the back row to the front seat, to lying on the floor (while trying to ice a corked thigh or another broken nose) and finally a promotion into the driver's seat when I obtained my Light Rigid class (LR) licence. I then had some more fun behind the wheel as the driver of the bus and to assist with all of the driving duties over the years of my playing career.

"Rabbits" was one of our early bus drivers. He was a legendary Royals bloke, whose real name is Peter Gallagher. Rabbits was the husband of Anne Gallagher, an amazing lady and dedicated volunteer to rugby, as well as an all-round amazing first aider. If you were injured or unwell, Anne would fix you up and if she didn't have the answer, Rabbits would apply tape to areas of the body that were not even required (just to shut you up). We all loved the Gallaghers, long time members of the Royals Rugby family.

Bob Shakespeare, a member of our early coaching and support staff, would also step in as bus driver when needed. He was another champion Royals rugby player and human. Bob's commitment to the team was outstanding, particularly given his marriage proposal to our number 8, Angel. These two legends went on to create a beautiful family including four baby Shakespeares and more amazing humans from the Royals rugby family.

Another of the bus drivers in my Royals days was Dave Cooke, the father of one of our youngest players Louise Cooke, nicknamed Cookie. I am unsure if Dave volunteered to drive for us to keep an eye on his underage daughter, as Cookie arrived on the scene at about 16 years old. Whatever the reason was, we all came to know and love Dave, whose daughter didn't marry one of the coaches but did go on to be one of the longest playing Wallaroos in the history of the forwards to that point.

What I tried "not to do" within these pages was single out specific players, otherwise this book would be double the size and you may need a spare pair of underwear for the laughing fits after reading about the antics some players got up to. What I would like to emphasis is, that from the front row forwards, to the wing and referee, from the half back to the coach and ladies in the canteen, every single player, whether on the field or not, played an important role in the history of women's rugby during my era. To you all, even though your name may not be recorded, I remain grateful.

Prior to the first tour to Newcastle, our team needed to decide on a name. Our name came about simply because about half of our newly formed rugby union team had come from the game of rugby league (which in 1992 had a men's national team called the Kangaroos). The other half were affiliated with the Royals Union Club (either a partner of one of the Royals men's grades or chasing one) whose national team name was Wallabies. After playing around with both men's team names, Loui and I (being the loudest members on the bus) decided on combining parts of both team names, Walla plus Roos equalled Wallaroos. It was that simple.

Many times, I have read an inaccurate story about the national Australian women's team name, where it came from and how it came about. The Canberra Royals Wallaroos (the original women's rugby union team to use this name) had no idea that there existed a very old (1870) Sydney men's rugby club with the exact same name. In the year 1992, we believed we had "created" the team's name which we Canberrans used for the first three years of the Newcastle Women's Rugby Tournament in Australia.

Readers will notice that during the very first international match played in the early '90s, at North Sydney, the Australian team weren't yet called Wallaroos. We played under the name Australian Women's Rugby Team. The reason was because the ACT were the owners of the name (the historic relevance was still unbeknownst to us as we believed we had magically created the name).

I cannot recall the exact year, nor the rugby camp (either '95 or '96) but Loui – my teammate and one of my closest rugby friends – and I were approached by Joan Forno with a request about our Canberra Wallaroo team name. Joan told us that the national body wanted the name to be used for our national women's team. This meant that Canberra would no longer be able to use the name if we agreed. As with every other request that Joan made, when she said "jump", we jumped, and agreed to hand the rights of the team name over to Joan and the ARU for trademarking. Although this was sad for our Canberra team, we kind of felt proud that our team name was going to be used for future national representative teams. Hopefully this information helps to set the records straight. To the best of my knowledge, none of the national team nor any of the early players were consulted on the name of the national team. This was a decision made above the level of our playing base. Today it is a true honour to see the team name embroidered on winter scarves, tracksuits and up in lights.

We don't know why Joan chose the name or whose request that was, but either way, this was what happened. In 1994, the team name would create some confusion around the August/September period when our ACT coach Col Spence was quoted by the newspapers as being the coach of the Wallaroos (which was correct). Col Spence (another legend of our women's game) coached the Canberra Wallaroos for years but never the Australian Women's Wallaroos (who, in 1994 were coached by another legendary Canberran coach, Mr Bob Hitchcock).

On the paddock

The "Inaugural Women's Challenge" of 1992 was the first time, in Australian women's sporting history, that a gathering of five teams of females, all from either NSW or ACT, came together to play rugby union. I believe a pause is required here. Please read the last sentence again.

History was made on the 6th of June, 1992. Women had finally made it to the rugby field (again) but in greater numbers than ever before. Thanks to the city of Newcastle and the local committee for hosting and organising this event. Thanks to the Australian Sports Commission and the Australian Rugby Football Union for the invitation to play. This event was the beginning of a life-changer for so many of us.

Three players from the Newcastle "Black-Butts" women's team posed for a photo which was used on the front cover of the program. Who would have ever thought that this photo and this Inaugural Challenge was the beginning of something so great for women's sport in Australia. What a privilege it has been for me to share these details with you and go back to some of the best years of my life.

The 1992 challenge was held at the Newcastle No. 2 Sportsground, National Park on Parry Street, Newcastle. Aside from what we really don't know from back in Sydney in the early 1930s in Australian women's rugby history, we do know that the majority of the five-team gathering in 1992 at Newcastle had never played rugby union before this weekend.

I will give a shout out to very old friend and player from the Canberra Royals Wallaroos rugby team, Franci Weyts, our vice-captain. Franci was an international student, living in Canberra during 1992. Franci responded to the initial invitation from Royals Rugby Club and turned up for training at Rivett Oval on her own. She had a love of rugby that was clear to hear and see.

Franci was the only woman (aside from Louise Ferris, who had played rugby in New Zealand as a child) in our entire team who had played rugby, in her adult years, in a female competition before we arrived in Newcastle. She became part of our team, was christened "Dutchie" and blended in nicely alongside Tracey Wilson in the 2nd row. These two ladies were about the same height and like most second rowers, became a solid hard-working unit on the paddock.

Franci had played rugby in the 2nd row in Holland for her own club side. She was a real gem for our team, and we were very happy to have her on board. English was her second language and we all "kind of" understood her instructions, except when she was lying on the bottom of a ruck and sporting her mouthguard, spitting and yelling at us in Dutch. I imagine these were frustrating times for Dutchie given she was surrounded by some clueless teammates. She taught me a lot in those early games, and I was grateful that she played in the forwards so I could follow her lead and learn quickly. I was keen to learn more about this new game and the laws from day one.

It is possible that players in the other four teams registered from NSW also contained players who had rugby experience from overseas. I do not know who they might have been or who they are until they too, write their own history and share the details with us.

Prior to the very first match, which was at noon on Saturday, the 6th of June, 1992, between the Newcastle Black-Butts and the Royals Wallaroos, we all had to attend and participate in a safety session at 10:30am. Although we felt like we were being treated like kindy kids, I thought this was a great idea. We were all keen to learn and safety is an important aspect of this contact sport.

It was also during this safety session that I became aware of Mrs Joan Forno for the very first time. Joan had a presence and a voice! She was a part of the safety session, she was a coach of the "P.M.T. Blues" and to be honest, she spoke with an authority that meant when Joan spoke, we all stood still and listened! There was respect for Joan from day one.

Other compulsory components of this challenge were that every player had to complete a written registration form. In the good old days this was done using a biro and ink (there were no online options in 1992 nor digital photos required)!

There was a compulsory fee of $5.00 AUD that had to be paid for insurance purposes and before anyone even participated in the safety session. I am unsure if I truly understood what I was about to risk going out to the field that day but at 20 years of age and amongst the new mates who surrounded me, I could not have cared less about any risk. We were all excited and keen to get the first game going.

Shout out to Michael V. Mahoney (insurance broker from NSW) who covered all female players that first historic weekend. Thanks also goes out to the ARU, who deemed that we required this instruction before that first head-high tackle (which came in that very first game down the left-hand side of the field).

NEWCASTLE, NSW

In hindsight, none of us realised the historic nature of our actions in the lead up to that weekend in Newcastle in 1992. Perhaps Joan Forno may have but we players were in it strictly for the fun and the good time with mates. Although many of us had played other ball sports in women's and mixed teams before, and at various levels, this was a first for us Aussies who were all adults and not stepping onto the field like the five-year-old girls of this current playing era in the history of sport in our country.

The real fun for me personally has been in the physicality and contact of the game. I loved both the attack and defence opportunities equally. Again, I could not choose which one I liked most. They both tested me in different physical and mental ways during every game. I loved the feeling of running as fast as I could whilst carrying the ball. Assisting the scrum and line outs were important parts of my position. But regardless of which part of the game I preferred, I always played to win and even when my body was physically tired at the end of a game, somehow I always seemed to find this inner strength inside of me which I believe comes from the mental aspect of playing the game.

I love the tackle (not so much being tackled). There is a sensation that comes alive inside of me when I am running toward an opponent, at my top speed and when I run straight into the body of the opposition player whilst attacking our line. I would hold onto that ball and protect it like it was something breakable that needed protection. I learned to hold it safely tucked under my armpit or held with two hands in front of my body whilst on the burst. One of my roles was to protect the ball and assist my mates in getting it over the try line. This behaviour was legal and within the laws of this game called rugby. It was the best fun ever! And physically it was the most challenging thing a human being did for fun, especially the feeling of fending off a player and running through that gap.

Alternatively, in defence, I would drive my shoulder, preferably my right but not always, to launch my body and full weight and speed into the abdomen of my opposition's body. My goal was to knock this player to the ground in the hope that in the process of my attack on her body, she might drop the ball or at minimum have to place it on the ground so I could try to steal it from her if I was still on my feet. The art of a great tackle comes with practice, although I do think that some players are gifted with this ability. Again there is nothing which compares to the feeling of a great and well-timed tackle.

By 20 years of age, my body had stopped growing (I only got to 161cm tall). I had spent these earlier years of my life playing either in the backyard of the family home, riding a bike and later engaging in various other team sports at different levels but never a national level. I had found my new home that weekend in Newcastle and "my tribe". Every training session during the warmup of this tournament and every game in the "round robin" that weekend felt just like Christmas Day! We had this amazingly talented team, three great coaches and this was the best fun ever.

In my very first game of rugby, I played in the forward pack. Matt Brennan had spoken to me about my role in the open side flanker position. I loved this #7 role from the very first game and the "job description" of this position. There was plenty of space for me to run and one of my goals was always to put as much pressure on the opposition five-eighth.

In those early games of 1992, the referee (I am pretty sure Joan ran onto the field at every stoppage too) would blow the whistle to cease play and talk both sides through the immediate infringement. We would all learn the importance of safety and body height, all the while reiterating the laws of this new game. A large huddle gathered in the middle of the field with the clock stopped so we didn't waste time that could be better spent trying to belt someone. In later years Bob Dwyer told me to "go get em and bash em". He also wrote this quote on a rugby ball that he signed for me whilst visiting one of our national training camps.

The referees that weekend worked harder than any other refs I would experience in my playing career. They must have enjoyed a few laughs at us all. I am grateful for their service to rugby, especially to our evolving game from this very inexperienced beginning. We all had a lot to learn, and I found the game of rugby more complex than league with more and different laws to grasp.

NEWCASTLE, NSW

Although in 1992 we played according to rugby laws set down by the IRFB, that weekend, there was one exception. We scrummaged using the U19 scrum laws. Effectively this meant that we were not permitted to push further than 1.5 metres. This was for our own protection and the safety of our necks and bodies (and so the insurance company didn't receive too many claims this weekend). We are bred tough in this country, but injury is a part of this game and every player's experience. I doubt there would be a rugby player in the world who escaped injury from training or playing this great game.

The weekend was a "round robin" format meaning that every team present for the challenge got to play against every team. The final would be battled out between the two top teams with the best performances during the challenge. The games were 30 minutes in total (2 x 15-minute halves) with a 5-minute interval at half-time. 20 players were allowed to be named for each game, even though most teams didn't have that many players aside from the Newcastle girls who had the advantage of being in their hometown (and registering girls they had found that morning in the shopping centres, pubs and elsewhere).

The players who were present at the first tournament in Australia include:

Canberra Royals Wallaroos:
Vicki Waters, Libby Andrews (argh that s!), Maxine Chessell, Tracey Wilson, Franci Weyts (Vice Captain), Jo Faulks, Helen Wylks, Genda Merritt, Louise Ferris (Captain), Carole Simpkins, Nicole Evans, Bronwyn Johnstone, Jenny Smith, Karen Aldons, Alison Smith, Karen Fitzgerald, Helen Taylor. Coaches: Matthew Brennan and Paul Cornish, manager: Wayne McAuliffe

University of New England (UNE) Earl Page College:
Jo Andrews, Lynne Turnbull, Meg McPherson, Danyale Juffs, Kelly Wilkinson, Kerry Daley (Captain), Pauline Olive, Emma Norris, Kath Chalmers, Mel Chillemi, Moira Litchfield, Kim Parsons, Gab Bradford, Linda Mortenson, Vanessa Franckin, Sylvia Wong. Coach: Troy Daley, managers: Katrina Milosevic and Wade Riley

Hawkesbury Agriculture College "Fillies":
Amanada Lingwood, Kate Clysdale, Kylie Robert, Lyndal Maloney, Rebecca Walshe, Mary-Anne Tulip, Kerris Ferguson, Pam Venture, Nicole Perrin, Lisa Graf, Jane Bred, Simone Munn, Kate Harris, Janelle Loosemere, Tanya Roy, Nicole Wilson, Coby Causer. Coach: Matthew Hood and John Cole, managers: Mark Challender and Andrew Ford.

Sydney PMT Blues:
Rebecca Hancock, Helen Price, Heather Turner, Julie Monro, Kathy McInnes, Moria Stewart, Anneka Chisholm, Michelle Ross, Christine Valentine, Lee and Gough (a full team list had not been provided at the time the program was photocopied, but I note a number of players in the PMT side remain anonymous and need to be found and added to our records when the next book is published). Coach: Joan Forno and manager: Diane Best.

Newcastle Black Butts:
Leanne Armstrong, Joanne Black, Caroline Blugg, Rachael Champion, Gina Chapman, Kirrily Cranstone, Sara Daley, Natasha Deaves, Cheryle Dedman, Vaness Dodd, Melissa Donaldson, Cheryl Dwyer, Carmel Falk, Sharon Foot, Susie Gillet, Karen Hassett, Leanne Hassett, Angela Holzhauser, Crystal Jones, Jane Lloyd, Nadine Lutherbarrow, Lesley Meldrum, Jo Murdock, Tiffany Munro, Helen O'Neill, Nadine Page, Kelly Scott, Jenny Tolhurst, Debra Tracey, Trish Walker, Monique Williams, Karen Wilson. Coach: David Porter and Mick Willis and manager: Janeta Barnes and Andrew Ford.

Canberra Royals Wallaroos were undefeated all weekend. After our win against those Black-Butts, we played and defeated Earl Page College at 2pm. On the second day of play at noon we also defeated P.M.T Blues (sorry Joan) then at 2pm we defeated the Hawksbury Fillies. The final was played at 3pm and our Wallaroos team got better and stronger with each game. Admittedly we made lots of mistakes, but we were all very keen to learn from these and improve.

We were on top of the world feeling so happy that we had travelled a great distance and were returning home with the first ever winner's trophy. It was fun and an absolute privilege to have been part of this first. To those early pioneers from Sydney in the 1900s who never got to play more than one game, nor even have their names recorded – that was for you girls too. I do have every intention of trying to name you in the one photo I have managed to uncover in our history records. The fun we had could and was shared amongst many.

The afterparty was held at the Ambassador Inn where we all enjoyed a buffet dinner and a few beverages. Ok, some of us didn't eat anything and just quenched the thirst after a weekend of games and some hot Aussie weather. Newcastle provided some great bars and other late-night establishments which were frequented by those of us wanting to party into the early hours of the following morning. There was plenty of mischief and loads of fun that evening and all the way home to Canberra on the back of the bus, the majority still very thirsty and keen to celebrate our win. Thank you, Newcastle, for hosting this inaugural event and for your hospitality too.

At the end of this first rugby season and as per my plan to head back overseas for more travel, I departed Canberra. Six months of absolute fun was had with a school mate Natalie, in the driver's seat of an old Ford LTD which we purchased in Boseman. Nat and I shared the driving, visiting all the American sites and places on our bucket list, stopping wherever and whenever we pleased. After spending my last dollar in the USA, we flew to the UK. I secured a job as a farm hand in Kent, England. It was lambing season and I found myself on yet another steep and fun learning curve. I was cooking for the family and workers, minding children, riding horses and delivering baby lambs when and if I ever got bored (which is rare)!

About one month into my farming experience, I caught a whiff of a women's rugby team called the Wasps. This club was located a short trip (for an Aussie) up the road from Kent. I managed to get a few runs with the club at training and a few games too. My eyes were opened to the fact that women's rugby was an established sport in England and had been played for years. There was more than one division of women's players, and this felt like an established competition just like the men's local rugby competition back home. This club didn't only have women in the teams, there were even young girls training and playing. This was a first for my eyeballs and I was amazed. I realised I was a long way from home.

A couple of months later, Loui Ferris and I would meet up again. Lou came and visited me in Kent and stayed on the farm before I packed my few items and headed across to Europe for a few beers during Oktoberfest in Germany. Those days remain a bit of a blur, but I know we did engage in some travel because I have some photos, just no memory.

During this period of my time on the continent, Loui and I reconnected with our old Dutch friend Franci Weyts. Not only did we get a run in Franci's Dutch club team, wearing the purple and white with words that made no sense to us, we travelled with the team to France and Germany where we played in a couple of women's rugby tournaments. I had some great fun with Loui and our newfound team, playing in Paris and beyond and learning more about the women's game and just how big the sport was overseas and in different countries around the globe. Regardless of where I went and played, I discovered that rugby people are similar in every country worldwide. Love of the game is one thing, love of each other and the culture that is part of it, is another. Half of the girls in this Dutch team could not even speak English very well but that made little difference to the connections that were made and the memories that remain.

Worldwide, I was learning that rugby people and the hospitality that they provide is similar no matter where you visit. The game on the paddock could be played for fun (which was never my style) or in fierce competition, which I would learn in years to come. Thanks, Dutchie, for your guidance in those early years of my rugby experience, for the fun times in Oz and Europe, the footy and the memories.

Loui and I went our separate ways after the tournament in Paris and my very first taste of red wine (which I mixed with orange juice in order to swallow)! It is still not my preference. Lou and another Aussie friend Janet travelled for a bit while I wandered off to explore the Eastern Bloc (and get away from all the tourists in Europe). I visited Poland, Hungary and Budapest before running out of cash and almost accepting a boat ride to Russia with a newfound travelling friend, but that rugby itch was present as it was getting closer to round one of the rugby season back in Canberra. I decided that Russia would have to wait and returned home.

1993

The second Annual Australian Women's Rugby Union Championship was held in Newcastle over the Queen's Birthday long weekend, on the 12-13th of June, 1993. This event included four Australian club teams, one team from Christchurch, New Zealand called "Kiwis" and one team called "Menagerie" who travelled all the way from Minneapolis, USA.

Both international women's rugby union teams became the first visiting women's club teams to play on Aussie soil. The distinguishing point was that both teams were representing their rugby club, as opposed to their state or country. Although NZ and USA had been playing women's rugby union in their own countries and abroad prior to 1993, during this championship we were all playing at club level. Our Aussie women's teams would have been the most inexperienced.

In 1993 it was a repeat of the same; the tournament in Newcastle had a name change but the location and timing remained as they were the year prior. The same club hosted the end of tournament presentation, but an entirely different mix of competition, talent and teams participated on the paddock.

The first game kicked off at 11.30am on Saturday, 12th June, when Canberra played Minneapolis. The other teams included Christchurch, Hawkesbury, Newcastle and Sydney. The final was played at 3.00pm on Sunday, 13th June, 1993 with the Wallaroos from Canberra being too strong for all Aussie teams for the second year in a row. We came up against Christchurch in the final but neither team could score even one point. It was a nil all draw. That game was tough, and we continued to gain confidence with each match even though we had not played a game since the year before at the same ground.

WALLAROO #19

The aim of this second tournament (as stated in the program) was to select an Australian side to participate in the upcoming Women's Rugby World Cup. We were encouraged to play as hard as we could yet the emphasis, like the year prior, was to enjoy the game and friendships that were offered.

Once again there was this heavy emphasis on safety. Safety sessions and instructions for all players was compulsory before taking the field to compete that year (although this was not as strict as my 1992 experience and those that felt they didn't prefer it, headed off to the toilet block or physio bench to avoid the opportunity). Personally, I thought this was a great initiative. The laws of the game were made crystal clear, and the referees were not mucking around with any of the safety aspects of the game. We Aussies were still barely out of nappies at this stage of our playing careers and the guidance offered was appreciated.

I was hungry for one of those Aussie jerseys that had been dangled like a carrot in front of me. Prior to the kick off in 1993 and during subsequent years when I showed up to play, I was on the hunt for a green and gold jersey. The thought of playing for Australia was tempting but would it be possible? I had never been in a position like this one before in any sport that I had previously played. It was exciting to be a part of this journey.

By the end of the 1993 weekend tournament, the strength of our Canberra Wallaroos team was evident. 12 players had been selected in the "Talent Squad", and these included: Maxine Chessell, Libby Andrew, Angel Rutter (Shakespeare), Tracey Wilson, Sharon Patterson, Jo Faulks, Louise Ferris, Helen Taylor, Margie Shelley (Brennan), Melinda Bell, Karen Aldons and Anne Murphy. Four additional players were also named in the shadow squad: Darlene Riley, Glenda Merritt, Jodie Bijorac and Cassie Smith.

My selection in this squad was hand delivered to me at the end of this tournament. It was printed on blue-coloured A4 paper, and my name was handwritten and mis-spelt (including that bloody s)! The congrats was signed off by Mick Willis and Rob Bradley on behalf of the women's subcommittee. That piece of paper remains stuck in my rugby scrap book. I notice it was the same, blue-coloured paper that was used the year before to print the program. Maybe it was a NSW thing? Maybe I was always destined for a career in policing?

Us Wallaroos drove south back to the nation's capital celebrating all the way home. A nil all draw in the Grand Final was good enough reason for us all to celebrate another successful visit to Newcastle. We felt good, had learned a lot and the tournament had brought as much fun as the previous year. Sadly, returning home meant there was still no local women's rugby union competition for us all to continue to play together. This was our journey.

Unfortunately, by July 1993, about one month after the trip to Newcastle, the story and support from the ARU had changed and significantly. Australian Rugby refused to nominate a women's team for the upcoming World Cup. The powers that be (despite the push from Joan Forno) insisted that we were not ready to compete at the international level (even though the ACT women's team had proved some strength by beating the US club side and the draw against Christchurch). We were unhappy with the news.

I felt demoralised. The lack of support from the ARU was upsetting and frustrating. At this time in our nation, our men's team, the Australian Wallabies, were afforded the privilege of travelling the world and were winning international matches, the recent World Cup and proving the rugby talent from our land down under – if you were male of course (I think I might have mentioned the patriarchy earlier?). We would have to suck it up and allow the "boys club" to call the shots, besides there was no option. We were used to this type of treatment given our sex and the state of play (in every aspect of life during this era of Australian history) if you were female. Things would hopefully change if we were patient enough and just continued to play for the reasons which we did. We would just have to wait for the men to give us a green light, it's just the way it was, they ruled the roost for the time being and there was no point complaining (even though we did)!

Joanne (Jo) Faulks was the representative for women's rugby in Canberra at this time. Jo tried communicating with the ACTRU and ARU only to be told that the ARU had made a decision, and it was final. That was unfair and a good opportunity for girls to return to the sports from which they had come. Many did and women's rugby lost some significant playing talent during these early years.

I had a visit to the game of soccer about this time. To be honest I had never played this game before so I thought I would give it a try in a social competition (except anything social for me was played competitively). The biggest issue I had with this strange new game was that every time this high ball came my way, I would catch it with my hands and start running.

My team got sick of me causing this repeated penalty, but I just could never resist catching the ball, I guess it was just inside of me from playing netball since the age of seven. For my whole life I had played women's sports where the ball was caught in the hands, not so much the feet. I was crap at soccer, it was not my game and I can admit that (even though I can admit it is another great game offered to women and one which continues to pave an amazing trail). I retired from soccer at the end of my first and only season.

In the lead up to that World Cup in 1994 which had been snitched away from us (and little did these men know, nor even Joan Forno), our little ACT band of annoyed players, via a contact in Holland and with the help of our old mate Franci, tried to nominate a Barbarian side (called "Convicts") into the World Cup. I still have a copy of the fax that was sent, attempting to register our Canberra Royals Wallaroos into the World Cup.

We felt that despite what the ARU were not prepared nor ready to do, we were all prepared to pay our own way to the World Cup and to organise and fund the trip ourselves (this was our normal). The passion for rugby was high and our enthusiasm to play on the world stage felt like it had been ripped away. Sadly, we had no joy; in fact, the entire 1994 Women's Rugby World Cup was cancelled at the last minute.

The original plan was for the Women's World Cup to be hosted by the Netherlands (which is where I personally sent our fax registration). But unbeknownst to us Aussies, it was cancelled just 90 days before the event was due to start! This was the journey of international women's rugby and to be honest, I am disgusted that we would be told one thing, and the opposite would happen. We were not children but grown adult women with a passion to play a game just like the men, yet the conditions were very different during these early years of establishing women's rugby in Australia.

A brave band of Scottish ladies, headed up by their Women's Rugby Captain Sandra Colomartino, stepped up to literally save the tournament. The sheer willpower, determination, passion for the game and some amazing assistance from so many turned this situation into a miracle for women's rugby. Had the Scots not made this effort for the game, who knows how many players, like the experience in Oz in 1993, may have walked away from the sport? The lack of respect and support by the ARU still baffles me and I still wonder why our game wasn't yet important enough to be developed given what was going on across the globe and for the years prior to Australia even getting the first tournament organised for women. My gut feeling at the time was that the men just wanted us to walk away from something they had invited us to in the very beginning. I don't know much about men, but I know this was unfair and frustrating. Again, we just had to suck it up and wait.

God bless the Scots. Thank you, ladies, for this massive effort and for all those helpers who got this show up and running. Your example was inspiring to us all. I am sorry that we didn't show up, we wanted to. In later years we would and even match up against the Scots (I even scored a try in our final game of the 2002 WC against Scotland).

We felt we had a lot to prove to the ARU and just wanted to play, for the very same reason every other player worldwide did. We loved it. Worldwide, women's rugby players were annoyed. The greatest of these were the Dutch and New Zealand sides which were banned from taking part (and maybe that is why those Kiwis want to kill opposition every time they play – no doubt they still haven't got over the treatment of their national players in 1994). It's a sad part of the history of our game yet needed to be included in my book.

Of course, the incentive for the Wallaroos was to train harder, get fitter and prove to the "decision and money boys" that we were serious about this sport and we wanted to continue to play. The ARU wanted to see us improving and developing our rugby skills and when they deemed we were good enough, they would let us know. I believed that the yardstick during this era was financial (maybe it still is?). How did the ARU expect us to play at a level that was good enough to attract fans and sell tickets in the grandstands to make a profit for the union, when we were not afforded the matches nor tournaments to improve our rugby skills and gain the experience required to play and win against the best in the world? Maybe the men were not ready to accept that Aussie women were going to be competitive, I am unsure. What I do recall is that it was it felt unfair to be treated differently to the men in every possible way. We didn't have anything more to prove aside from the fact that we loved the game and wanted to play too.

It was then the ARU announced that in place of the World Cup, there would be a three-match tour of a New Zealand Team late in 1994 with the view to a reciprocal visit by NZ later. It was a consolation prize but it was better than nothing and something for us to be grateful for and work towards.

The first of those, as you know from a previous chapter, did happen. After this test and the end of the 1994 season, I decided to leave the sport. This was due to personal reasons, namely a relationship break up with a team member which was hard for me to navigate. I decided that a "geographical" was the best option for me during this period of my adult life while I nursed a confused and broken heart and needed a clean break.

The following year whilst I was learning the ropes in paid employment in WA, the Wallaroos crossed the ditch for the first time and toured New Zealand. Games against three provincial teams in the South Island, Mid Canterbury in Timaru, Otago in Dunedin (at the House of Pain) and Southland in Invercargill were played.

In Newcastle, 1993, there were six teams registered to play with two of these coming from overseas. This was exciting and it had never even occurred to me that teams would travel so far to compete but why not. The after party was equally as good fun as the year prior, however before the music started to play, there was an announcement and when Joan Forno spoke, we all listened. Future chapters contain more information on the events of each annual tournament.

At the end of the 1993 Newcastle tournament, the first ever Australian Women's Development Squad was announced. Players included: Kim Taylor (Qld), Karen Aldons (ACT), Margie Shelley now Brennan (ACT), Angel Rutter now Shakespeare (ACT), Sharon Patterson (ACT), Tracey Wilson (ACT), Maxine Chessel (ACT), Jo Faulks (ACT), Helen Price (NSW), Shelley Lingman (NT), Libby Andrew (ACT), Helen Taylor (ACT), Helene Corthals (NSW) Florrie King (NSW), Glenda Merritt (ACT), Kelli Thompson (NSW), Claire Nichols (NSW), Rachel Simpson (NSW), Kelly Scott (NSW), Sharon Foot (NSW) and Tiffany Munro (NSW). Coaches were Mick Willis (NSW) and Paul Cornish (ACT & an ex-Wallaby), assisted by Rob Bradley (ARFU).

In July that same year (and while I continued playing league on weekends for East Canberra), I received my first ever communication from the Australian Rugby Football Union Ltd. The letter arrived on official ARU paper and was dated 12th July, 1993. It had been one month since I had heard my name read aloud. This communication "sealed the deal" and made the opportunity more real than just hearing my name. I was excited!

1993 Australian Women's Development Team

NEWCASTLE, NSW

The contents of the official envelope were bulky. In addition to the letter was a training program that had been formally approved by the ARFU Executive Committee. I was encouraged to follow the program if I wanted a jersey and had dreams of playing in the first Australian Women's Rugby Union Team. Ten members of the team were Canberra players so I wouldn't be short of a training buddy.

Details of a camp scheduled for October 1993 were included in the communication, along with the request "for squad members to cover their own transport costs to and from Newcastle". The ARFU had generously offered to cover the other remaining expenses (accommodation, meals, and kit). Things were changing in the women's rugby space, and this was big news for us girls. I had three months to get fit, adhere to the program and prepare for my first ever commitment to the ARU. I was keen to improve my fitness and skill and impress at the camp. The dream of that Aussie jersey was becoming real.

By October 1993, the current rugby league season with East Canberra had come to another successful end. I was fortunate to still have rugby league in my life, my match fitness was maintained, and I was like a crazy woman with determination when my hands felt that ball. Regardless of whether it was league or union, I was hungry to play and get fitter and stronger. As East Canberra Ladies we won another Grand Final that year and I felt like I was the happiest girl in Australia. My life was carefree and was all about footy, training and game day. I lived, breathed, and loaded myself with good food and rest in preparation of the camp.

I worked hard on my fitness. I also got busy to ensure that I knew all the laws of rugby union game (besides, I didn't want to drop another ball over the try line!). I undertook a basic referee's course which taught me a lot about the laws of our game. I even started watching rugby on TV. I have never been one for sitting down too long, so I started to get into this game and learn all I could while pushing myself to become the fittest I had ever been. The pine forest at the top of Renmark Street became a place I would run long distances. I had always been good at sprints and hills but never really enjoyed distance running. The average distance that a player in my position at open side flanker would cover in each game was about 7km. Of course, I had to run 10km just to make sure I was training harder than those other flankers wanting my spot on the team.

During this period of my life, I was single. I was living at home with my parents, the same parents who today have been married for nearly 64 years and are still supporting me, and me them.

The majority of my siblings had grown up and moved out of the house by 1993 (although it seemed that people just moved in and out with the change of seasons). I had a bedroom to myself, which was not my normal as a kid growing up in a house filled with nine humans. Good old Mum had dinner cooked every single night when I returned to the house, excited to share my day with my two parents, yet physically exhausted.

On the morning of day one of our training camp, Friday, 29th of October, 1993, I rode my bike about 90km along the Federal Highway, from Canberra to Goulburn. I have always been a keen bike rider and for whatever reason, I was filled with nervous excitement that was best sorted on the saddle of my pushy that morning. I knew the Royal bus was heading to Newcastle via Goulburn and would stop at the regular location for #1 toilet stop, so I couldn't resist racing the bus to Goulburn and releasing some of my nerves.

The girls in this first development team participated in the camp from Friday evening at 7pm until 3pm on Sunday, 31st of October, 1993. During that time, we engaged in various classroom sessions, fitness testing, skill testing, nutrition, sprints, strength training and paddock sessions including our introduction to scrum, lineout, and something foreign to me called "backline play"!

The camp was physically and mentally demanding. There were numerous classroom sessions which required paying attention to a range of coaches and staff who joined us. Cathy Horton, Tracy Willis, David Manson, Max Dednam, Mick Willis, Joe Dunnage, Rob Bradley and Paul Cornish, all helped out that weekend. I felt grateful and excited about the opportunities which were heading Australia's way. That weekend exposed me to things

I didn't have a clue about yet but which would all become familiar in the coming years (topics like nutrition and diet, sleep, recovery, and so on). It was a privilege to have been part of the very first gathering of baby Wallaroos. These were exciting times. We had progress!

My pushy and I caught a ride home to Canberra on the bus that Sunday afternoon. I reckon I must have slept the whole way home. Although we didn't yet have a team name, the Wallaroo journey had begun. That felt exciting.

1994

This was the trifecta year for women's rugby in Newcastle. The third consecutive year that the annual tournament had been held in Newcastle (an Australian town known for coal and coal export). As a new game for women, we were gaining momentum even though competitions were not yet established in the states around the country. The speed in the development and the increased interest in our game continued to grow. It was exciting to be a part of this era.

The 1994 tournament was badged "Australian Women's Rugby Championships". It was for the last time held in Newcastle over the June long weekend (11 and 12th June, 1994). The programme this year I noticed was printed in colour and the paper used was upmarket in comparison to the previous two years. I am unsure if the tournament was sponsored given that the program read "International Rugby Review". Apparently, the program was now a "souvenir programme" and players like me had to pay $2 for a copy. Change was coming and this came with a price tag apparently.

Joan's constant presence was felt, and she was already dubbed and voted in as the President of the AWRU Committee, a sport which had now grown to five Australian states and included more than 500 participants. Rugby was here to stay, and the future was looking promising and positive. A whopping 15 teams had turned out for this annual event in 1994. Three pools of four teams and Pool D limited to three teams only. Woohoo, this was real growth, there were new players everywhere which was super exciting.

Pool C contained a returning women's team from Christchurch (the majority being the same players we had tied with the previous year in the Grand Final). These ladies were the only international players registered for the tournament in that year.

Our Canberra Wallaroos team remained mainly unchanged. Some players left and were replaced but this was usually due to pregnancy or work transfer as opposed to a change of mind. Of course, sometimes girls were injured too, which prevented players from returning to this contact sport. My experience was that once girls got a grasp on that Gilbert, there was a hunger for more, besides it is a great game, suited for all different shapes, sizes and personalities. There was a position for everyone, even if that resulted in non-playing team members because we needed reliable support too.

The standout development in the 1994 tournament was the expansion of the participants and teams registered for this event. Fifteen teams included: North Queensland, Newcastle, Souths (Brisbane), Sydney University, Waverley (Sydney), ACT Wallaroos, Norths (Brisbane), Kiwana/Sunshine (Qld), Wests (Brisbane), Northern Territory, Southern Cross University, Christchurch (NZ), Hawkesbury (Fillies), Easts (Brisbane) and Sunnybank (Qld).

The ACT Wallaroos team of 1994, in which I played included the following teammates: Belinda Todd, Glenda Merritt, Ronnie May, Tracy Wilson, Sharon Patterson, Joanne Faulks, Libby Andrew, Angel McGurgan, Louise Ferris, Helen Taylor, Darlene Riley, Louise Barron, Margie Shelley, Anne Murphy, Karen Aldons, Anna Willock, Fiona O'Brien, Sarah Haigh, Jodie Bijoriac, Christine Rogers, Maxine Chessel and Genevieve Job. Our coach was Col Spence and Bob Shakespeare, Manager Lannie Pomazak, Sponsor Peter Pomazak. Sport Trainer was again the amazing Ann Gallagher.

Sadly, 1994 would be our last visit to Newcastle, and even worse those bloody Kiwis would strip my team of our winning streak. The ACT Wallaroos were defeated by Christchurch 13 – 5 in the Grand Final. It was time for the tournament to develop further and time for the venue to be shared around our nation. What is obvious to me looking back in those initial three years of the annual tournament, is that registered teams were all clubs as opposed to state teams (meaning the club teams were not the strongest players coming from that state). The playing pool, in any location around Oz, was not large enough to field a "state" team and the early tournaments were filled with the most inexperienced of players. Of course, they had to be as we had never played before 1992.

Finally, for the first time in the history of the women's rugby union game in Australia, the final was refereed by a woman. Carolyn Warren had participated in the competition in 1993 but had not been privileged (or maybe considered not experienced enough) to hold the whistle for the most important game between the most experienced teams. It was great to see the expansion and development of the women's game, extended also into the official roles. Carolyn would become a familiar face and participate in many of the tournaments nationally and internationally in my playing career over the coming years.

The future national women's rugby union tournaments would be hosted by:

Canberra (1995), Sydney (1996), Adelaide (1997), Darwin (1998), Perth (1999), Canberra (2000) and the locations varied until 2017 with the Australian Women's Championships held somewhere around this nation annually and between state representative sides (not rugby club teams like we experienced in the early days of women's rugby in this era). From 2018 the Championships evolved to the 'Super W' competition as we know it today, with five Australian teams aligned to the men's Super-Rugby competition.

During my research for this book, I would learn, all these years later that Australia was advised that there would be no funding for the event as a women's WRC, as it was not sanctioned by the IRB. As an IRB member union, we were obligated to follow their directive (which of course we would do, especially with Joan at the forefront). Both the 1991 and 1994 WRWC's were originally not recognised by the IRB, and those two World Cups were only subsequently recognised in 2009 in the IRB records.

5

FIRST INTERNATIONAL TEST

The first official international women's rugby union test played in Australia, on the 2nd of September, 1994, was a battle between Australia and New Zealand for the Laurie O'Reilly Cup. Mr O'Reilly was the first coach of the New Zealand Women's National Team and a major advocate for the women's game in New Zealand.

Prior to this historic international test in Sydney, the NZ Black Ferns would play in two warm up games, the first against the Canberra Wallaroos team in the nation's capital. The second match would be played against the NSW Blues at UWS (a university field in Western Sydney). This NSW team was a combination of the best NSW players or those that were available and brave.

The entire playing team of New Zealand women were billeted amongst our Canberra women's representative team. I personally had never brought a billet home throughout my entire childhood and in all the sports I had played. My brothers had brought plenty of billets home from Marist College during their teen years, but this was a first experience for me and possibly for my billet too. Billeting was a great way of getting to know the opposition, their culture and for reducing team costs.

WALLAROO #19

Some of my Canberra teammates took two billets home. This was due to the fact that some Wallaroos were still students in high school and were unable to take home a giant and hungry athlete for a few nights! This first hit out was about having some fun and seeing if we could compete in women's rugby internationally.

Unbeknownst to me, my billet was one of the team's wingers. Louisa Wall #11. When she alighted from the bus and I saw the sheer size of this walking, smiling woman, I wondered if we had mixed up the wingers with the second rowers! I wondered if I would physically survive the rugby game in a few days' time.

Fortunately for me, I would not be lining up opposite Louisa on the paddock. She was in the back line, and I was a part of the forward pack. I was relieved and terrified in the same moment. I welcomed her into my crappy little car (an old Mitsubishi Gallant sedan with little leg room for my giant billet) and drove her home, chatting all the way and not feeling awkward at all.

Louisa spoke with a strong Kiwi accent. I liked her instantly; she was easy going, sported a huge smile and just seemed to fit into my family home and the routine on Renmark Street. I love my billet even though I hated what she did to my team during this first game in Canberra, the second game in Sydney and every game in which we would meet over the coming years. New Zealand were just too good in my playing era, they were an amazing team full of talented sportswomen.

The first warm up game for the Kiwis was played at 12:30pm on Friday, 26th of August, 1994 at Manuka Oval, Canberra. This was the first time a women's rugby union game was played against an international visiting women's rugby team in the history of our Canberra and Australian women's rugby history. The local Canberra Wallaroos girls (being a team of state representatives as opposed to international level players) matched up against the New Zealand National Team. The referee was Peter Marshall, an international Australian and IRB referee.

FIRST INTERNATIONAL TEST

The ACT Wallaroos team was comprised of: Helen Taylor (Captain), Louise Ferris (VC), Louise Barron, Karen Aldons, Jody Bijorac, Anne Murphy, Sarah Haigh, Fiona O'Brien, Glenda Merritt, Bronwyn Johnston, Sharon Patterson, Ronnie May, Vicki Waters, Cassie Smith, Angeline McGurgan, Margie Shelley and Libby Andrew. Our coach was the amazing and dedicated Col Spence. Our equally amazing manager and sponsor was Lannie Pomazak (Pete was of course on the sideline and nearby too)! Family and friends, members of the Royals Rugby Club and local rugby supporters intrigued about this game turned up to spectate. This was probably the biggest crowd I had played in front of during my union career. It was exciting.

The New Zealand women were coached by a female, Vicky Dombroski, with Assistant Coach Darryl Suasua and Manager Leo Walsh. Their team was filled with legends including: Geri Paul, playing numbers: Geri Paul, Lauren O'Reilly, Tracey Lemon, Fiona Richards, Nina Sio, Rochelle Martin, Davida White, Helen Littleworth, Anna Richards, Jacqui Aplata, Tasha Williams, Lenadeen Simpson-Brown (captain), Vivienne Rees, Louisa Wall, Monique Hirovanaa, Heidi Reader, Natasha Wong, Eva Epiha, Julie Reynolds, Jude Ellis, Regina Sheck and Liza Mihimui. Many of these faces would become familiar to me over the coming years, some playing full 15-a-side rugby as well as the sevens game like I did.

Admission to the game was $2 for adults and $1 for children. A 10-a-side girls curtain raiser was played before the international game. The Canberra Wallaroos were the current Australian Champions and held this title for three years running, ever since the annual Newcastle tournament of 1992.

Prior to this game, the Canberra Wallaroos had played a total of 20 games. We had won 17, lost 2 and drew once. No Australian women's rugby team had ever beaten us – at least, not until Friday, 26th August, 1994! It was time for our local Canberra Wallaroos to come back down to earth and be beaten by a better, stronger and more experienced team.

A recall of this game is required even though I prefer not to think about it and prefer even less to write about it, because this book is about the history of our game in Australia and my own rugby reflection. I will allow the pain of that game and its memory to return.

One thing that no one playing that day from either team could forget was the cricket pitch that was in the centre of the rugby field (that oval is used for many sports but primarily for cricket and AFL as well as rugby). That cricket pitch was unforgiving and as hard as concrete. Minutes into the game, the referee decided that any play possible needed to be moved off the pitch to reduce injury to the players which assisted in keeping some skin on our knees, legs and bodies. If a scrum was required on the pitch, the referee moved the play to a couple of metres off where it should have been. What a sensible ref this bloke Peter Marshall was on the day, we all felt grateful. This had never happened in any other game I had played in nor after this one ended.

ACT were defeated on the day by a truly amazing team of NZ women's rugby players. This game was played at a level that we had never experienced thus far in our limited playing careers. The Kiwis ran in 15 tries to nil (which sounds less painful to me than a final score 87-0). Ouch, that's all I can say. I could not keep up with the pace of the game nor the experience which oozed from the forwards as well as the backs. No doubt Those Kiwis enjoyed this first hit out in Australia.

It's just my opinion, but Anna Richards, at first five-eight as well as my billet, Louisa Wall, were the superstars of game. The entire NZ team were impressive. Congratulations goes to the entire team and coaching and management staff. Now, we knew what defeat felt like and it was a feeling we would start to get used to whenever these black jerseys arrived at the stadium.

Anna scored two early tries early in the game. The scoreline was 17-0 after only 17 minutes of play! By half-time, the score was 36-0. Monique Hirovanna at full back wearing #15 scored three meat pies, slotting into the plays of her back line and pulling off some moves that even we Wallaroos enjoyed watching from the other end of the field. Leeanne Atkins wearing #14 on the other wing was impressive as was their entire and scary forward

FIRST INTERNATIONAL TEST

pack. These were gifted athletes and there was no mucking around, they were present to win and that was obvious to all.

Anna scored another two tries in the second half of play. My billet Louisa grabbed a total of four tries, running all over the field, including the cricket pitch and over the top of every Wallaroo on the paddock. Thank God that game ended, it was the longest game of my life!

A couple of days later on Sunday, on the 28th of August, 1994, all Wallaroo hosts delivered their billets back to Royals Rugby Club, Weston to wave them off for 10am departure to NSW. We had some homework to do before the International Test in less than a week. Six of our Canberra Wallaroos would head to Sydney to prepare for the International Test Match against this same team. These were Helen Taylor, Louise Ferris, Libby Andrew, Margie Shelley, Angel McGurgen and Ronnie May (my first female partner).

On the morning of the 28th of August, the six of us beaten and bruised Canberra Wallaroos joined the rest of the Aussie team at the NSW Academy of Sport at Narrabeen, Sydney. State players arrived from all corners of the nation to prepare for the Test Match that weekend. The video recording of the ACT vs NZ slaughter provided the whole team and coaching staff with some valuable information.

That Monday, the 29th of August, our national team played a practice match against the NSW Under 16 boys at Rat Park, Warringah. This was the most evenly matched competition available to our women's side throughout our nation and about the same playing level (even though those young men were fitter, faster and more skilled than us). I often wondered how those young men felt matching up against our first women's national team. It was a wonderful opportunity for us to have a game and a practice run together, something we will always be grateful for lads. You young men did us all a favour and did yourselves proud.

On this same date, at the Hawkesbury Agricultural College, Sydney, the New Zealand ladies played their second game against the NSW Women's team. NZ defeated NSW, with a final score of 85-0. Sadly, I was not present to witness this game. Perhaps it was for the best as it is painful watching your own teammates defeated by the same team who had literally run all over us in Canberra less than a week before. What I do know is, the NZ Women's Rugby Team from those first games were amazing and our state representative sides were no match for the best they had brought across the ditch for this first ever international tour to Australia.

On the Wednesday morning of our Sydney rugby camp, the team to play the Kiwis was announced: 1. Karla Clay, 2. Bronwen Hart, 3. Ronnie May, 4. Nicki Wickert, 5. Angel McGurgan, 6. Deena Aiken, 7. Selena Worsley, 8. Yasmin Stafford, 9. Louise Ferris, 10. Helen Taylor (our captain), 11. Kerry Davis, 12. Bronwyn Calvert, 13. Angela Doidge, 14. Kathy Beitzel, 15. Angela Fairweather, 16. Julianne Columbus, 17. Pearl Palaialli, 18. Robyn Chambers, 19. Libby Andrew, 20. Tina Chapman, 21. Sharyn Williams and 22. Margie Shelley. These numbers represent not only the team and our positions for our first international game but also the number that was assigned to each of us. These numbers commenced the history records for Australian Women's Rugby Union history records. We were coached by Mick Willis, assisted by Paul Cornish and managed by the wonderful and talented and much-loved Christine Gold (Goldie).

On Friday morning, the 2nd of September, 1994, we left the Academy at Narrabeen and transferred to a hotel closer to the ground in North Sydney. Our accommodation was the Centra. We enjoyed a light team walk before heading off to the ground for the biggest game of our lives (well maybe the first of many of the biggest games of our lives).

This international women's rugby union match was won by New Zealand 37-0. Our national team had performed better than the two Australian state sides in the lead up games to this international and thank God the result was not as embarrassing. My memory of this game is not as sharp as others so I will leave this opportunity open for the next Wallaroo to document a commentary about this first loss in the international arena. Losing was tough but history was finally made and the women's game had taken the first of many steps that would be required to continue the sport into the future.

FIRST INTERNATIONAL TEST

Our first ever Australian Women's Rugby Union Team had been defeated, along with the two state teams in the warm-up matches. New Zealand were outstanding and played at a level well beyond the capability of our 1994 Australia national team. The NZ ladies returned home across the ditch with the Laurie O'Reilly Cup, and on the 3rd of September, 1994 it was all over. We all went home to our respective states and countries to enjoy a rest (for a few hours anyway).

The next day, Sunday, the 4th of September, 1994, I backed up for East Canberra and played in my very last rugby league Grand Final, bruises and all. Showing up for my club team (rugby league) along with the teammates who had done the same provided me with a good opportunity to run out all those frustrations! Besides this was my "normal" and finally that weekend, I grabbed the ball and ran like buggery once again. For the final time, I felt what it was like to win a rugby league Grand Final. It's a great feeling and a great game which I loved playing all those years.

My football commitments for this year of my life were over. It was time for a rest. On the 17th of October, 1994, I received a little gift in the post from Joan Forno (President of Australian Women's Rugby Union). The post pack contained a letter from Joan on ARFU letterhead. Joan sent her personal congrats to the entire team who represented Australia in that first Test Match.

Joan included three items in the parcel that were unable to be distributed during our camp in Narrabeen (these being an Elizabeth Arden make-up kit, a Pierre Cardin wallet, and a team photo). It was a lovely gesture. Good old Joan Forno, still working hard behind the scenes and trying in any way to ease the pain of the loss of our first international game. Regardless of the scoreline and the walking wounded, we all knew how proud Joan was of us.

At the end of 1994 I decided that I had achieved what I had set out to do as far as rugby was concerned. I was 23 years of age and had wandered into a career opportunity which I wanted to explore. I had undertaken some training with the Australian Protective Services in Canberra, and had volunteered to head up to Western Australia to take on what felt like a new challenge for me in the "paid career" arena, an area I was yet to discover given footy had consumed most of my early adult years without financial income.

At this time, in Australia history, we were receiving an influx of "boat people" (illegal immigrants), entering our country or attempting too via our northern shores and borders. By January 1995, I had commenced my first uniformed shift with the Australian Protective Service (APS), working at the Port Hedland Immigration Reception and Processing Centre (IRPC). My role was officially as a member of the security team, and we were to ensure that none of the "residents" absconded from the facility over a barbed wire metal mesh high fence nor tried to escape or harm themselves. I had pretty good priors for chasing and tackling people, so I came into this role with plenty of tools in my personal kit. I had never lived in WA nor even travelled to that part of Australia prior to signing up for this position, so the world was once again at my feet and excitement and new challenges awaited me. My backpack, pushy and I got busy again, chasing new challenges and new friendships.

I felt the right time for me to take a break from footy had arrived. Although I felt disappointed to lose to the Kiwis, I will admit they are an outstanding force and on the rugby stage are always going to be a challenge to beat. I knew I had been a part of something very special and felt satisfied with my own personal effort and the achievement that being a part of the first Women's Rugby International Team had brought to my young adult years. It had been a privilege.

1995 – 1997

My new interest in paid employment and working at the IRPC was fun, exciting and challenging. This period of my life enabled me to explore parts of Western Australia that I had only seen and read about in books. I was on a steep learning curve, communicating in Cantonese, getting to know the residents and loving my life. My work shifts were 12 hours per day, yet I often worked overtime which made for a healthy bank balance – not so much a healthy work-life balance. Shift work and I got on well. I rode my bike to all the places I needed to attend, and I loved my job, my work mates (well most of them) and the workplace. Most of all, I was learning more about myself too.

Within that first 12 months of living in Port Hedland, I wound up playing for the representative mixed touch footy team (1995). While playing in a tournament in Perth, about 1600 kilometres down the road from my new hometown, I met some women from the Western Australian Women's Rugby Union Representative Team.

Before I knew what had happened, I was reading my name printed in the WA representative side to travel to Canberra for the 1995 National Women's Rugby Union Tournament. This was the "new face" of the Newcastle Challenge which I had played in for the previous three years (and the sport which I thought I had walked away from but was somehow magnetically attracted to again). Being offered a #7 jersey for a different Australian state was a temptation that I was unable to resist.

This would be my first time representing another Australian state in a women's rugby team, which felt kind of weird given I had played my entire rugby career out of Canberra and wearing the jersey with our nation's capital's coat of arms and two swans. The WA rugby kit was predominantly black and yellow, and I am guessing it was the black swan that made me feel ok with defecting from my home state.

My life was exciting and fun. Rugby for me during this period was strictly social, a contrast to the sheep stations as well as all the training I had done in previous years to prepare for this same annual tournament. I made some good mates and had some great times in Perth but realistically, I lived 1600 kilometres from the training field and this would be a "one-off". It was a privilege to be invited to play and I thoroughly enjoyed the experience.

During the 1995 rugby year, the development of our Women's National Team continued. This was the first year where the Australian Women's National Team would tour to New Zealand. Our girls played in three provincial games in the South Island, Mid Canterbury in Timaru, Otago (at the House of Pain), Dunedin and Southland in Invercargill.

Like the previous year when the NZ girls toured to Australia, the players from the selected teams were billeted into the homes of the NZ girls for the South Island games. Then they flew to Auckland to play the NZ ladies in the Laurie O'Reilly Cup for the second time. The team were to play in the curtain raiser game to the Australian Wallabies v New Zealand All Blacks, however, sadly, the venue for the game was changed at last minute due to the heavy rain which fell the night before.

1995 - 1997

My mate Loui and I flew across the ditch with a small group of supporters to be present at this second Test Match between our enemy and to witness history being made. The Kiwis were again too good for our inexperienced team. The ground was wet and muddy, and the final score was 67-0. I travelled back to my life in Port Hedland, kind of starting to miss playing in the mud and fun and wanting to have another go at trying to defeat those Kiwis. Neither Loui nor I appreciated watching from the sidelines that tour and although we had some fun and didn't have a care in the world, we both wanted dearly to be out on the paddock with the girls.

The Port Hedland chapter of my work and sport life was amazing and super challenging. The job at the IRPC was up and down, filled with trauma, rooftop protests, extractions and long, long shifts. I worked hard and really enjoyed my role. Within that first 12 months, I had saved enough money to put a deposit on my first investment property buying a small fibro home in Port Heddy. I loved Western Australia, the heat, the work, the travel and the beauty of this part of our nation. I learned a lot and made some mates who I still keep in contact with today. I found myself in a new relationship with a lovely guy from work called Tony. We made some great memories together and he was a sweetheart and a great and dedicated officer at the IRPC.

For personal reasons, by the time St Patricks Day came around in 1996, it was time for me to return to Canberra and support my family. It didn't take long for Ferrit to track me down and drag me (willingly) back to training.

The word on the street was that Australia would be sending a national team to the 1998 Women's Rugby World Cup in the Netherlands. A familiar feeling instantly arrived back inside of me, the excitement and anticipation of rugby and now, the challenge of an international tournament overseas. No one needed to persuade me to play and re-sign for the Canberra Women's Team in 1996. I could not return to the training paddock quickly enough. I believe my body had enjoyed a break from the routine of training and I was more excited than ever before about the possibility of playing for the Wallaroos overseas.

Newcastle had hosted the women's rugby tournament for those first three years. Canberra hosted in 1995 when I was a player in the Western Australian Women's team and now, I was preparing for a return to the tournament in Sydney (1996) with my old Canberra teammates and getting myself back into a fit state to compete seriously. I wanted one of those Wallaroos jerseys.

Pete and Lannie Pomazak, our trusty ACT sponsors, were still dishing out the money to help the team cover costs (God bless Pete for all the cash he injected into ACT Women's Rugby and league). I made the cut to represent ACT at this tournament and we were off. I had my favourite number 7 jersey on my back and on the June long weekend we headed off to play at Rat Park, Sydney. Selections for the national squad would be made following the Grand Final of that tournament so it was perfect timing for me to return to rugby after my adventures in WA.

1996

The Australian 1996 Women's Rugby Union Championships were held from 15-20th July, 1996, at Pittwater Rugby Park (known as Rat Park), Narrabeen, NSW. The majority of Australian states and territories were represented (all bar Tasmania). Queensland beat our ACT team in the Grand Final 30-5 and the level of rugby and experience within the women's ranks was rising. Those Queenslanders were big and tough and too good for us Canberrans. Women's rugby in Australia was in a stage of big growth, and it was exciting to be a part of it all again. The improvement in the standard of play was high and obvious both for us players, and for the spectators.

Being selected for the Australian Wallaroos after my performance in that 1996 Sydney tournament was a big deal for me. We were two years out from preparing for our first ever International World Cup and I felt privileged to be invited to train with the national squad. I knew it would take a lot of hard work to make the final cut for Holland, so I decided not to return to paid employment. Instead, I had a chat with Loui and talked to her about my dream of being a full-time rugby player.

1995 - 1997

Ferrit and I were of the same mindset. She quit her job in the public service, and I didn't have one to quit. Loui and I would meet at the local Royals Training Oval every second day, if not every single day. We had access to the gear in the training shed and basically wrote our own fitness and preparation program, with the help of a champion Royals and ACT Academy coach, Andy Clarke.

Loui and I belted the crap out of each other and those tackle bags at Rivett Oval, running an endless number of dusty hills and concrete stairs at the back of Chapman, swimming laps, weight training at Deakin and undertaking our own skills work. Loui tried to teach me to step too but I never, ever got it – it's just not in my genetics!

In August 1996, Australia would again host the third-ever play off for the Laurie O'Reilly Cup. Another Test Match between the New Zealand ladies (now called the Black Ferns) and the Australian Wallaroos was fought. We were defeated again, this time managing to actually score one try against what was an incredible team of talented female athletes 28-5.

1997

March 1997 came around and I was invited to join a team of Australian women to play in the Invitational Hong Kong Women's Sevens. We could not register or play as the Australian Women's Sevens Team as the ARU would not recognise us as an official Australian team. How we even got the invitation remains a mystery if we were not permitted to play under our nation's name nor official colours. The players of this very first sevens team were not selected from trials more as players who were selected by management and offered a place on the team and members who could secure sponsorship, scholarship or raise their own funds to participate. The ARU direction during this period of our growth was to concentrate on the 15-a-side game. Therefore players, coaches, management, funded their own opportunity to be part of the first women's sevens tournament in Hong Kong. I have no idea how or why I was selected to participate, I can only assume it was from the 1996 Wallaroo squad. I will say I was very excited at this opportunity to play sevens, a different version of rugby that I was highly suited to playing.

The ACT Academy of Sport had previously offered me a scholarship due to my national selection in 1996. These staff assisted with my training programs, fitness testing and coaching. Andy Clarke became my coach and although he could not attend Hong Kong (nor was he invited), I give credit to Andy for helping me out with my preparation for my first tour to Hong Kong. I was fighting fit and mentally as ready as I could have ever been.

The Hong Kong International Women's Rugby Sevens (HKIWS) hosted the first ever tournament for women. All games were played at one location, Aberdeen Stadium, over the weekend of 15-16th of March, 1997. Massive thanks and congratulations goes out, across the miles from Australia, to a female player, administrator, volunteer, Maria Allan (Chairwomen of the HK Sevens Women's Committee of 1997).

Hail Maria and her team of volunteers (also women's rugby sevens players), who included but would not be limited to: Sue Pace (Secretary), Charlie Cullen (Treasurer), Sue Slater (Sponsorship), Keri Glenday (Player's liaison), Pippa Hoctor (PR & Marketing), and Vicky Harris (Grounds). Huge thanks and congrats goes to these ladies and the un-named volunteers working in the background, assisting to get this first amazing women's sevens tournament off the ground, 21 years after the men's game got started in Hong Kong. Again, this was another huge milestone for women in the rugby union code and globally.

In March 1997, 12 nations participated in the first women's rugby sevens tournament. Since then and aside from the COVID-19 pandemic (and the absence of this tournament in 2020 and 2021), the event has gone from strength to strength every single year. From an amazing beginning, look where this tournament took the game. Women's sevens in 2024 continues to impress the world audience, showing off the talent of the women's players that waited so long to be given this opportunity to blossom and show off the skill of the female rugby player.

1995 - 1997

In 1997, the grandstand where the women played was occupied with only a handful of spectators (and the players from the other nations who were enjoying the break in between games). There was no crowd, there was little following, and this was our beginning. It is amazing to see just how far we have come and to witness the sold-out crowds of this modern-day game now even played at the Olympic Games.

The 1997 Australia team was represented at this tournament under a team name called "Aussie Gold". Players consisted of: Elizabeth Andrews (I have no idea why my name was printed this way as I would prefer Libby Andrew, but I was happy to make the program and team), Bronwyn Calvert, Wendy Packer, Vanessa Nooteboom, Sharon O'Kane, Tanya Osborne, Naomi Roberts, Helen Taylor, Nicole Wickert and Selena Worsley. Coach: Mr Bob Hitchcock, Manager: Mrs Joan Forno, Physiotherapist: Jenny Birckel and sponsored by: Qantas, Canterbury Australia, and Pauls Milk, QUF.

1997 Hong Kong Sevens

WALLAROO #19

The invitation to participate and my selection for this first ever women's rugby sevens team arrived, in writing on the 20th of January 1997. This was only eight weeks before we flew out of Australia.

I received my official confirmation via facsimile (fax) from our Team Manager and President of Women's Rugby in Australia, Mrs Joan Forno (see website libbyandrew.com.au). For those readers born post the 20th century, the fax machine is a method of communication and was a modern device of the time. In 1997 it was a handy and efficient way to communicate. My dad had a home office, and his precious fax machine was about the size of a refrigerator and parked up in the lounge room of our family home. In those days, the messages were printed on glossy paper in which the ink would disappear after a few weeks if not months. Anything that I wanted to save (which included all my records), I would photocopy and glue into my expanding scrap books.

My participation in the Aussie Gold team would come with a few costs to me. Firstly, all team players were required to fund their own trip. Joan had asked each player to pay a total of $1,300 AU to cover some of the expenses. Secondly, we would all be required to take paid leave.

The request to fund my own participation was not new to my experience playing any women's sport, nor did it impact my decision to accept an Aussie Gold jersey (which was in fact a dark shade of navy thanks to Joan's beautiful husband and generous donor Allan). I did not hesitate for one second. It was a privilege to have been invited to be part of this team. I felt pumped with adrenalin, and I had signed and returned that fax to sender within minutes of receiving it. Thanks, Joan, for all the organising and in your own time.

Fortunately for me and as a result of the influence of my dad (an accountant who raised and paid all expenses to put his seven children through catholic education, food, clothing and support a wife), I had some dollars saved in the bank. I was 26 years old, feeling young, fit, injury-free and busting with excitement at the thought of visiting my first Asian country and playing a sport that I absolutely loved.

1995 - 1997

Rugby Sevens is a very different game to 15-per-side. My talents on the field went hand in hand with this game, I was one of those players that kept running despite being too exhausted to run any more. Somehow, I always found that extra bucket of energy inside me to push me to keep on running, keep on defending and refusing to give in to the challenge of any opposition.

The Australian Rugby Union (ARU) had given us permission to participate in the international tournament, so long as we weren't called Australia. It was a strange experience given none of us could hide who we were, the way we dressed, nor our Aussie accents.

Regardless of what the ARU wished, we arrived in Honkers as "Aussie Gold", wearing navy blue and yellow jerseys rather than the green and gold like the men were privileged to wear in the big stadium across the park. These lads enjoyed a few extra privileges than we did but our team were grateful for the evening we got to spend with the Australian men's sevens team on their harbour cruise sponsored by Australia Banks in Hong Kong.

Joan Forno had worked hard behind the scenes to get the cost down as low as possible and collected small amounts of sponsorship money which all helped us to fund our own tickets. A big thank you to Allan Forno who paid for our playing kit, most of our meals out, our medical kit, the team's oranges and bananas and general needs during the tournament.

I felt super excited and proud to have been selected in this inaugural team. There were only ten jerseys up for grabs and I read my name in the team list (usually up the top given my surname starts with A). I stepped up my fitness and skills training in preparation for the tournament.

During 1997, Mark Sinderberry was the General Manager of ACT Rugby. Upon announcement of this first ever women's sevens team, three women from the ACT (myself, Helen Taylor and Sharon O'Kane) had been chosen. This was pretty big for Canberra given there were only ten players selected from the entire nation. The other standout fact was that we all hailed from Royals Rugby Club, Canberra.

Helen, Sharon and I unexpectedly received a generous donation of $500 AU from Mark and the board, to assist us with the cost of participating for the Aussie Gold team. I am guessing that our local Canberra Union might have felt sorry for us having to pay for our own expenses, but I am unsure. I did find a letter dated 6th March, 1997 in my treasure chest, which I had sent to Mark after arriving home from Hong Kong, thanking him and ACTRU for their kind donation and wishes.

My Canberra teammates (Helen, whose nickname is 'H', and Sharon O'Kane, known as 'SOK') and coach Bobby Hitchcock all departed together from ACT. We were joined in Sydney by the remainder of the team from other states including NSW, QLD and NT. We all headed out of Oz on the 12th of March, 1997. The tour was for one whole week, with the tournament being played across the weekend of 15-16th March, 1997. We returned to Canberra on the 19th of March, 1997.

Note: the original team selected to represent Aussie Gold 1997 included a talented athlete and great rugby player from Darwin (NT) by the name of Angie Doidge. I remember Angie because she was fast (and I was challenged physically by any back line player that could beat me in a foot race). She also stood out because she was an NT player, and these were a minority in the national sides.

An issue for Angie arrived in between the period of time that the team was selected in January and the scheduled departure eight weeks later. Pregnancy. As excited as Angie was about the pregnancy, we were all sad that she would miss the tournament. Pregnancy is one of those "women's issues" unique to women's sport and that baby and the timing of the pregnancy was perfect – not so much for the team, but a miracle for Angie and family. As Angie withdrew from the team, Wendy Packer from NSW excitedly packed her bags and joined us at very late notice. Congrats to both ladies, especially Angie.

The Aussie Gold Team, along with every other nation participating in 1997, was accommodated at the BP International Hotel on Austin Road in Kowloon. It was a great location and all players and management from

1995 - 1997

every nation stayed there. Some of the teams did not speak English as their first language, but we all enjoyed the atmosphere and comradery. It was an absolute hoot to have us all under the one roof. Team photos were staged on the same day at the same time, a bit like primary school photo days, trying to wrangle a large bunch of children and get them to all stand still. For me, that's what rugby is all about, enjoying a new experience, new mates, and connecting with people on and off the field. The Hong Kong 1997 tour was a fantastic experience.

On a daily basis for that entire week, we would meet up with opposition at the breakfast bar or in the lift. The atmosphere in that hotel was electric. I will never forget being a part of that first tour to Hong Kong, it was magnificent and probably my favourite of all four sevens tours of my playing career.

We landed ourselves in Pool A with Japan, Holland, England, Canada and New Zealand. The Pool B teams included: Fiji, Singapore, USA, Scotland, Arabian Gulf and Hong Kong.

The first two days of our tour to Hong Kong included lots of light training, working out our plays, moves, positions and combinations. We rode the local and jam-packed subway to get to the training venue each day and learned a lot about the Hong Kong culture. We didn't do much but train, eat and sleep in the lead up to the tournament.

Joan was just like a surrogate mother to us all. She was a brilliant manager and a highly organised lady. We all had great respect for Joan (and to be honest were pretty scared to step a foot out of line while she was about). We were all familiar with and fond of our coach Bob Hitchcock. There has been no greater man nor coach in my involvement with the game of rugby.

Our first match of the tournament was at 9:40am on the Saturday against the Poms. We had heard on the international grapevine that these fit-looking female athletes were the best in the world (they had won the 1994 Women's Rugby World Cup – 15-per-side – defeating the USA). God only knows how many of their 15-a-side World Cup winning team took the field that morning to shape up against us, but we had absolutely nothing to lose. The game was tough. We fought as hard as we could, but we couldn't match the experience of these ladies. We lost our first game 10-7. Joan made us honey sandwiches on white bread following the match and we were all forced to eat a banana as we warmed down and listened carefully to Bob and the wise feedback he offered.

At 11:00am we came up against the NZ "Wild Ducks". Although we had priors with NZ in previous Test Matches from 1994 onwards, we had never matched up against their international sevens team. These girls were outstanding, the ball and stepping skills were amazing and Tasha Williams (NZ national female sprinter) carved us up. Credit goes to NZ Wild Ducks and their coach who defeated us 29-0 – that hurt! Again!

Two losses in a row was not the start we wanted to the tournament but hey, this was a first and we were learning with each game. It was also obvious that the Kiwi girls were not playing under their national banner either. Like us, they weren't wearing their national jersey nor any type of fern. I guessed these ladies were fighting the same battles as their ANZAC buddies across the ditch.

After lunch and another hot honey sandwich, at 2:00pm we played against Canada and grabbed our first win of the day, 24-5. The final game of day one was against Holland at 4:40pm, another win for Aussie Gold, 43-0. Unfortunately, our two early losses and a somewhat lopsided pool saw us miss the chance to make it to the Cup Playoffs.

On the Sunday, we played at 9:40am against Japan and kicked butt, winning the game 46-7. We proceeded into the Plate Semifinal against the United Arab Emirates and won convincingly, 41-0. Our only hope of glory was to win the final game of our tournament and steal the game from Canada who had also made it to the Plate Final. We won this game 17-7; a great result for our first time appearing on the international sevens rugby circuit.

1995 - 1997

Joan was happy and thank God, no more honey sandwiches would ever be offered to me again! I don't like honey, but I was too scared to tell Joan that I would have preferred dry bread or a banana sandwich.

There were no surprises in the Cup Final, the Kiwis were too bloody good for us all. A presentation was held at 5:00pm and we finished the tournament absolutely buggered yet satisfied with our performance. Aussie Gold got better with each game and full credit goes to our support crew, our partners and family who came to witness this first international sevens extravaganza for women.

We had this amazing presentation dinner for the players and staff on the 16th of March, 1997 at the Kowloon Cricket Club. Another unexpected invitation for me loomed that night. I had been selected to play in an exhibition match on Day 2 of the Men's Sevens World Cup at Hong Kong Stadium. I am unsure how I landed on the team list, but we guessed that it was the eight tries I had scored across the weekend during the tournament. The highest try scorer of the tournament was the Kiwi national sprinter with 10. I followed closely behind with 8 tries (not too shabby for a loose forward).

This "invitation" would be the first time ever that women were permitted to play on that main field inside that massive Hong Kong Stadium. Woohoo what a thrill it was for me to not only have been selected but to be able to represent Australia in the barbarian team (of course not wearing any green nor gold to identify me)!

The match took place on Saturday before the men's first game. I was part of the 10-girl barbarian team called "The Rest of the World". We matched up against the Hong Kong Women's Sevens Team, wearing a maroon jersey with some Asian writing embroidered in blue on the left breast and we all wore our own nations shorts and socks. I had swapped my playing shorts with an English girl at the end of the tournament, so I was completely in disguise (until my name came up in lights on the huge screen at the stadium).

WALLAROO #19

The Rest of the World Team was comprised of four Kiwis, three Yanks, two English Roses, a lone Scottish Thistle and me, the only Aussie and all the way from the Royals Rugby Club in the nation's capital! The atmosphere in that stadium was something I had never experienced before. It was electric and scary and exciting and amazing all at the same time. I was nervous. My partner Sharrin was right there on the sideline (water runner for our team) and the stadium was packed and noisy.

The game got started and within the opening minutes, I had scored the first try of the match! It was the first try any woman would ever score on that paddock (well maybe it was less a paddock and more a lush green rectangular field). Regardless, it was a huge privilege and definitely a career highlight.

The weirdest thing was scoring that try and jogging back to the halfway line and seeing myself up on the big screen. I felt embarrassed! It was a new experience and the longer it went on, the more awkward it felt. I hadn't come all that way to be on the TV screen and it felt uncomfortable. I decided to run faster so the experience would pass. The first try and even receiving that ball from a teammate felt surreal. That moment was the greatest end to the most fun I had ever had in a rugby tournament worldwide. Maybe this was also what rugby heaven feels like. Words can't describe how I was feeling and the mix up of so many feelings in the same moment.

Fortunately, the game of sevens is played at a fast pace, and we were out to win. I got back to the halfway line as fast as I could given I was still gasping from the breakaway try. Our team went on to win the game against the Hong Kong Ladies. The final score was 42-0. A few beers were had and Sharrin and I hung about in the huge crowd enjoying the men's games and getting amongst the celebrating. What a brilliant end to my first tour to HK.

The local Canberra comp started up after Easter 1997 and we continued to travel to Sydney to participate every weekend in the Sydney Women's Rugby Union competition (playing for the Jack Scott Cup).

1995 - 1997

The 1997 Annual Women's Tournament was held in Adelaide, South Australia. This tournament was important in the lead up to the Holland World Cup. One wee spanner in the preparation for Adelaide was my 5th broken nose. The weekend before we were due to leave for South Australia.

Having a broken nose was tricky. My confidence was lower than usual, and it was decided that I should wear a brace. A special "nose guard" was hand-made for me, to protect my nose and face during play. The guard did bring me some confidence, sporting those two black eyes upon arriving for our first match but the comments from the sideline were a bit difficult for me to ignore. I was labelled the "Hannibal Lecter" of the Adelaide Tournament and many of my teammates from other states requested a photo with me wearing my absurd but handy guard. I didn't break my nose again that whole tournament and fortunately, I was selected in the squad to train on for World Cup. Holland here we come.

Hong Kong Stadium 1997: HK V's Barbarians

WALLAROOS FIRST WORLD CUP 1998

Before we get into the Wallaroos' first World Cup year in 1998, I need to take you back to the June long weekend of the year 1993, in Newcastle NSW. This year and state hosted the annual rugby union tournament for women in Australia. It was the second occasion of a gathering for 15-per-side women's rugby union players. Four Aussie teams participated: Waverly "PMT Blues", Canberra Royals "Wallaroos", Newcastle "Black-Butts" and Hawkesbury "Fillies", there was also one team from Christchurch called "Kiwis" and a team all the way from Minneapolis in the USA, known as "Menagerie".

It was this tournament and the performance of the Aussie girls which led to the selection and announcement of the first Australian Women's Development Squad. I heard my name called amongst a crew of excited others. This is where my international rugby journey commenced. I realised that opportunities to play at a higher level would come and this game was about to get serious. I was as keen as mustard.

WALLAROO #19

It was shortly after this gathering in 1993, that I was introduced to a player from the Northern Territory. Her name, Shelley Lingman. She was a tall, blonde, kind of typical prop size, athletic woman (which in lay girls' terms is the kind of scary and intimidating variety, especially when they are running towards you at full speed)! The weird thing was (or not), Shelley spoke with a Kiwi accent. Bloody Kiwis! They were everywhere in Australia but so long as they were on my team, I welcomed them.

Shelley and I started out as "teammates", wearing that same first green and gold jersey and part of the same forward pack. Shelley in the front row and me in my favourite position, open side flanker.

In the years to come, in addition to being a player's wife, rugby player, mother, rugby mum, grandmother and boasting many other talents, Shelley would gain qualifications and experience as a level 3 rugby coach (which in our country is the highest achievable level for any coach in this sport). Congrats Shelley on a wonderful playing and all-round rugby career. You are a star and were a huge asset to women's rugby in Australia.

Fast forward to 1998, when we had the opportunity to play in our first ever International Rugby World Cup, and Shelley was still part of the team like me, yet her role had expanded, matured and progressed into that of assistant coach. She was a passionate and talented coach and had been guided by one of the greats, Mr Bob Hitchcock.

Shelley was a "Top Ender", meaning that she lived in the top end of our country. The capital city of the Northern Territory is Darwin, and this is where the invitation sent to all Wallaroos came from. This was the invite which would change the course of my life.

The year prior, during the annual Women's Rugby Union Tournament, was when I fronted as 'Hannibal Lecter' in Adelaide, South Australia. At the end of each annual tournament, the national team was selected and announced. This was the year that anyone aspiring to play for the Wallaroos at the World Cup in Holland needed to be playing their best rugby to be selected.

WALLAROOS FIRST WORLD CUP 1998

In 1997, Shelley Lingman was the president of the NT Women's Rugby Union. She and her band of local NT committee volunteers had a brilliant idea at the end of the nationals in Adelaide. Armed with their copy of the list of Wallaroos' who had been selected for the World Cup, they commenced weaving some magic.

Shelley spread the word in Adelaide that the Darwin Women's Rugby Union was seeking players and an offer for all Wallaroos would arrive in the coming weeks. True to her word, Australia Post delivered the envelope to my home address. This contained a personally signed invitation, a small purse containing $200 to assist with travel expenses and the offer/opportunity of a lifetime.

There were originally 40 girls selected in the World Cup training squad, which would be cut back to 26 before lift-off in April 1998. The offer from Shelley was to travel to Darwin to "come and try" the lifestyle, play rugby in the women's top end competition and gain match fitness in preparation for the World Cup. It was a smart initiative and the first time an offer like this, in the sporting landscape, crossed my life path. I was keen. My commitment to rugby and my position in the Wallaroos Squad was one of my highest priorities at that time in my life.

The Darwin ladies competition is played at the opposite end of the calendar year to the majority of Australian playing rugby states. This is due to their monsoon season and weather patterns in the top end of Australia. This effectively meant that you could play rugby on the East Coast of Australia in your usual local competition from about April/May through until October and if you took up the Darwin offer, you could literally continue playing rugby for the entire year. That way, players could maintain match fitness until mid-March of the following calendar year (if your body could handle that kind of physical beating and of course the heat)! It seemed like a great opportunity for me and amazing preparation for the Women's Rugby World Cup.

The offer came (possibly from Shelley's home printer) signed with a silver ink pen. The final paragraph of that invitation read "accept our offer and find out just how unique top end rugby is. Come and give it a go – who knows, you might even like it and stay."

I had no idea at the time I accepted this invite that my partner and I would do just that, stay for a few more rugby seasons, a couple of new careers, extensive travel to all corners of the NT and remain there for about 12 years I love the Northern Territory and I loved the opportunity to travel and learn as much as I could about this magnificent country, my home Australia.

An old 1984 NT tourism advertising campaign in Australia returned to my head along with the catch phrase: "If you never never go, you will never never know". At the time of the campaign, I was only 13 years old, but I never ever forgot those words or the images of some of the most beautiful, rugged scenery our country has to offer. What a thrill it was to be a part of this World Cup campaign and the lead-up to another overseas adventure.

My golden ticket had arrived, a bonus $200 AU to help with fuel expenses and my dream of visiting NT was only one YES away. Thanks Shelley and the NTWRU Committee for this invite. It was time for another geographical change, this time including my new partner Sharrin (who had moved from Queensland to the ACT for work in the same year I arrived home from Port Hedland). I had an amazing experience in the never never and will never never regret the decision to accept the offer.

Once again, I was packing my backpack and preparing to head off for another adventure. This time it was not for paid employment nor requiring my passport but for a sport which I loved more than any amount of dollars.

Sharrin didn't hesitate to quit her retail job of seven years with the Michael Hill Jewellery chain. At the time, she was the company's top selling sales employee and female manager in Australia, but she was ready for a change of environment, was young and energetic, and keen to explore the NT too. Sharrin and I had met each other at a rugby ground in Sydney six months prior to departing together for NT.

WALLAROOS FIRST WORLD CUP 1998

On Boxing Day in 1997, we affixed our mountain bikes to the back of her little Holden Barina, threw in two backpacks, a pair of footy boots each, two sets of headgears into the boot of her car and headed off to the Never Never (without air conditioning and just over 3,000 kilometres still to travel via good bitumen road)!

My parents had gifted us a road map of Australia and waved us off from the Andrew family home in Duffy. It seems hard to believe that back then there was no such thing as Google Maps and I didn't even yet own a mobile phone (nor needed or was interested in one)!

By early January, 1998, we had arrived safely in Darwin and had stopped to visit many new sites and states along the way. I have always had an interest in history, and there was a lot of it to learn and so many interesting places to visit. The trip was great fun, but I was keen to get into training and start my preparation for the World Cup. I still had to make the final cut! I knew there were plenty of girls wanting my potential position as flanker, but they would have to get past me first and I was (and still am) a determined and competitive customer.

My life in Darwin for the next six months revolved around training at Marrara Rugby Park, the oval at the South Darwin Club and the surrounding suburbs. Sharrin and I were both assigned to a local club called South Darwin, which had a women's team in need of some experience and numbers. We fronted up for the first training session and were surprised to find the team in warm up mode, drinking cold beer inside the clubhouse and laughing and joking around (not geared up in footy boots nor mouthguards at all). This was a sight I had never seen before (and I refer to pre-training not post), but this was the top end, a place where life revolves around a cold beer or iced coffee milk, mixed with laughter and mates.

I became the captain for the Darwin Women's Team and led by example from the first hit out at training. We had a coach, typical of many women's teams which I played in, who was the partner of one of the players. Darren was our coach who continued to turn up every training and game but closer and closer to the cold drinks than the field, while Sharrin and I taught the team what we had learnt in the few years of our playing experience.

Sharrin took on the role of sports trainer as well as playing half back in our South Darwin team. Needless to say our club was pretty happy with Shelley Lingman (who scored two players from the south), a Wallaroo in the forwards and a bonus half-back who over the next few seasons would take on the coaching role also. Sharrin and I were a package deal and a great combination for many years in many respects too. South Darwin was a wonderful club, and we had some amazing times and created some wonderful memories during those years spent in Darwin. Our team had some great success along the way.

The women's rugby subcommittee in Darwin during those '90s was active (like all southern states at the same time). Shelley Lingman headed up the committee with other amazing ladies including but not limited to Shirley Russell, Maree Young, Angie Doidge (who had delivered a healthy baby boy), Kristen Richardson, Gail Barlow, Dallas Campbell, and Naomi Roberts.

Due to the Women's Rugby World Cup scheduled for May 1998 in Holland, there was no repeat invitation to the Hong Kong Rugby Sevens tournament. Every country sending a team to Holland was either concentrating on the 15s game and or saving their dollars and participating in some rigorous fundraising.

I stayed put in Darwin and devoted my life to preparing for the World Cup. I was 27 years of age, and I had very few commitments outside rugby. This was rugby heaven for me, totally committed and enjoying every moment.

"Paid" employment in Darwin came easily for me. I have never struggled to find work and have always been open to giving new things a go. Within days of arriving in Darwin, Sharrin and I had found a town house in Millner. We moved in with barely any possessions aside from a car in the designated car park and a few items which spilled out of the two backpacks. We signed a rental agreement for six months and, for the first time, moved in together. We got busy searching the positions vacant in the local newspaper for employment. It was an exciting time of my life. I found the climate similar to my years spent in Port Hedland; cyclones came and went, and the heat was a factor I loved.

I started work during that first week of my new life in Darwin. I landed a full-time job at the Alawa Gym (Darwin suburbs and only about 5km from home via a bike path). I was responsible for opening and closing the gym each day. I had a range of duties which were familiar to me, like writing training programs for clients, signing up new members and testing their fitness, cleaning the equipment and gym, making the protein shakes and selling the range of products that were offered. The owner of the gym was a laid-back local bloke called Phil who worked the evenings. Phil and this job were both gold.

I would religiously open the gym at 8am (after I had done my own training at 6am and ridden to work). At noon the gym would close for two hours for the "Darwin siesta". I am unsure why, I guess it was the God of my understanding, but the gym opening and closing hours were ideal for my World Cup training. I had full use of the gym equipment too.

At noon, every weekday when I locked the gym, I would get back on my pushy and ride 5km to Nightcliff Pool. After swimming 100 laps of freestyle and having a stretching session followed by my packed lunch, I would jump back on my pushy, ride another 5km back to the gym and re-open for the afternoon clients. Life was simple and uncomplicated. I loved the challenge of rugby and my commitment to preparation for Holland.

At 4pm on weekdays, it was knockoff for me. My trusty pushy and I would head across to Marrara for club training two nights per week, where I would do it all again (fitness on Tuesday and skills and drills on Thursdays). Games were on Saturday afternoons in the heat of the afternoon and Sunday was a day of rest and time to thank my higher power I had not died yet of exhaustion nor become injured as so many were every week. The heat could be intense for those that were affected by it, and it was common for a player to race to the sideline to vomit in between penalties in Darwin. Heat exhaustion and dehydration were both risks of playing any sport in the top end. Thankfully, neither were issues that affected me.

Rugby injuries at both training and during games became part of the norm. I was fortunate to escape serious injury throughout my career, but I can't ever forget that sound on the main oval at Marrara one Saturday afternoon when a great friend, Natalie Scown, playing for Litchfield in the black and red, broke her femur. The sound of her leg breaking was loud, and it happened so quickly (probably not for Nat). I will never forget that game, it was probably the worst rugby injury I would witness. Gosh Nat was tough, a beautiful life-long friend and hard and committed rugby player.

Teammates were injured often, just like the men. Knees and ankles were twisted and torn, collarbones were broken, and the odd concussion was suffered. Injury was part of the game and trainings too.

Looking after my own body was a part of my rugby that I took seriously. Icing small niggles, stretching, warmups and warm downs were all done religiously. Sleep and diet were important to me too. These were all new concepts that I learned in that first Aussie Women's Development Camp way back in 1993 in Newcastle, and developed across my playing years.

I will say 30 years on since that first international match, there is probably another entire book that could be written about the state of the women's rugby body post a playing career and the range of complaints that my mates and I have experienced. I, however, wouldn't change what I did for quids, it was all worth it and the fun and memories certainly outweigh the pain (at 52 years of age anyway). I have no physical complaints, aside from lower back issues to highlight (and this could only have been compounded by four occasions of childbirth) nor want to frighten off newcomers to the great game of rugby.

My first season playing for the South Darwin Women's Rugby Union Team was enjoyed thoroughly. By the end of March, we were done, and things heated up as the Wallaroos Squad was cut to a team of 26. I had made the team and my training, increased match fitness and game experience had all improved along with my fitness and strength. I was heading to Holland and was super excited.

The Australian Wallaroos flew from all states across our nation and gathered in Sydney prior to heading to Holland. It was during this time, when most of us were the most excited we could possibly be, that some sad news landed. One of our most experienced and greatest players, Helen Taylor, our #10, had decided to withdraw from the World Cup Tour.

Helen's beautiful mum, Jill, had been battling breast cancer and had taken a turn for the worse. Although it was a decision that had to be made, there was no hesitation from H. The arena in which she was most required was beside her dear mum's bedside. I felt sad that Helen missed the tour, we all did and she was greatly missed in the team and on the field. Helen was one of the toughest and one of the dearest training buddies of my Canberra rugby days from 1992-1997 and an amazing human and friend.

Helen played at five-eighth and was the short little menace that somehow could always get in front of me at training. In many respects she was the rabbit, and I was the greyhound. She pushed me hard and I continually tried (as hard as I could) to catch up to her level of fitness. Helen inspired me and without great players like her surrounding me in those early Royals days, I doubt whether I would have got to Wallaroo level. Helen, Loui, Margie, Angel, Jodie, Murph, Whoppie and many others had come across to rugby from touch footy. Those girls filled our backline and the forward pack with amazing talent. Their touch and oztag skills taught us all how to play as well as they could. Their standard was high and together we all stepped up into a platform that really was amazing.

Our forward pack equally was filled with amazing players like Max, Toddy, Glenda, Kristy, Ronnie, Tracey, Rookie and so many more that I don't want to single out for fear of excluding anyone. Together we made up a team and without every single player, we would not have achieved what we were able to do. They were great years of my life that's for sure. Lifelong mates were found and those friendships and parties (and funerals) continue to re-unite us all.

WALLAROO #19

Sadly, Helen missed the tour to Holland but was present with her mum to hold her hand as she passed from this life into the next. Helen didn't play again. She is considered, in my opinion, one of the best players and team captains to ever to wear the green and gold (H was actually there before we were even afforded that privilege)! After a short gathering in Sydney, and with our replacement five-eighth kitted out (Helen Theunissen), the Wallaroos, coaching crew, and management team departed on the 26th of April, 1998, via Singapore to Amsterdam. We were booked in and stayed at the Hotel Akers Loot.

The opening ceremony was at 7.00pm on Friday, 1st May, 1998. All teams gathered to join in the Dutch entertainment and welcome, followed by game one of the tournament. The Netherlands team played Canada in front of a crowd of about 1700. History had been made, the Canadian team had won 16-7 and there was a wealth of women's rugby awaiting the world over the coming two weeks.

Our first international game outside of our own country in the 15-per-side game was against the Irish Women's Team. It was played on Saturday, 2nd May, 1998 and was historic for us all, including Ireland, who would get the first taste of the new kids on the block and the first hits and tackles too. We had arrived. Prior to this hit out our Wallaroo team had only ever played against the Kiwis and USA at this international level.

We really had no idea if we were going to be competitive. We knew we had enough courage to give it our best shot, but our standard of play was unknown until that first match where Australia finally showed up.

History was made for Australian Women's Rugby, and I give credit to Joan Forno for the constant battles to get us to that first Women's World Cup. That day was an emotional one especially given some of us, like me, hailed from places like Cork, Ireland in the 1800s when our ancestors fled Ireland to Australia (escaping the deadly potato famine). Who knows? Half of the team might have been related to us given the amount of Irish who immigrated to Australia in our first 200 years (but that's another story). We snatched our first win against the Irish 21-0 in a tough battle.

WALLAROOS FIRST WORLD CUP 1998

We were on the score board with our first win under our belts and a whole lot more to learn. For our first experience ever, we didn't have to face those Kiwi girls and their Haka, but instead listened to Danny Boy sung over the stadium microphone. We had finally made it to Holland and the tide had turned.

Game 2 came around just three days later on the 5th of May, 1998, in a battle against the Frogs (whoops I mean France). This team on paper had loads more rugby experience than us and had been playing for years (in excess of 100 given their records go back to the 1890s)! Honestly, I don't think any of us really thought we would be able to compete against teams coming from the Six Nations, but we had nothing to lose and a lot to prove. We went down by two points during this game, losing to the French ladies 10 points to 8.

After a welcome three-day break, a few pool sessions, stretching and some down time on a bike ride through the tulip fields, we backed up for our third game against England. This game was played on 9th May, with the final score 30-13 in England's favour. These girls, like the French, were miles ahead of our skill, fitness, and knowledge of the game. They seemed huge, they had skills beyond ours and experience that oozed confidence. I will admit, we were not enjoying these losses yet needed to put our experience into perspective and just soak up the experience and gain all we could from these early defeats. We were fit and enthusiastic, not so much experienced, nor did we have enough knowledge of the game to beat quality sides like the Poms. Well done ladies, we were learning what would be required in the years to come.

Game 4 came around, and thank God the Spanish arrived on the opposing side of the field (finally a team from outside of the Six Nations arena). We finally were able to make the most of our opportunity and got another win on the board. It was the 12th of May when we grabbed our second historic win of the tournament. It was a close, hard-fought game with a final score of 17-15. We all felt much better and satisfied after this win. It certainly gave us a boost of confidence going into our final game, the play off for the "Plate".

WALLAROO #19

We knew that Scotland would be hard to beat, since they had been playing at least ten years prior to us. This match would be our final one on Dutch soil. It was a race to finish either 5th or 6th place overall out of the 16 nations represented. Scotland were the first to score before we drove to a 13-10 lead at half-time. Two more tries were added to our scoreline before the full-time whistle blew. The score was 25-15 and we were awarded this beautiful silver plate. Thank God we had something to gift to Joan Forno after all the hard work she had put in, along with every single member of the squad. It had all been worth the effort.

Coming out of the World Cup with a silver plate was huge for us Wallaroos. Although we wanted to win the World Cup, realistically we were kidding ourselves given we were probably the most inexperienced team in the competition. We had nothing to lose, a lot yet to learn and a truckload of games yet to play to gain the experience that we would require to become competitive in future international matches.

At this period in the history of our game in Australia, funding was tight and hard to come by. A player like me, who took this event seriously, had quit employment to attend the tournament overseas. Unpaid leave for a period of six weeks was the "norm". This was 1998 and the majority of the Wallaroos had, like me, prioritised their rugby and disregarded the financial losses. The gains to our self-esteem and mateship as a team were enormous and definitely worth the sacrifice. This game called women's rugby was the best fun a girl could find. It was physically and mentally demanding and tested my attributes in ways that I never anticipated. For this experience, I will always be grateful.

Some of the Wallaroo team were in full-time employment, which meant applying for leave. If awarded this could be paid up to four weeks' pay, with the rest of the period being unpaid. Here in the land down under, many full-time workers are only entitled to four weeks leave per annum. Some of the players were mothers who had no income at all and needed to leave their children and families back home on the opposite side of the globe. Other Wallaroos were students with little or no money for travel expenses nor any form of luxury. Either way, in my era, we certainly

WALLAROOS FIRST WORLD CUP 1998

did not play for the allowance which we were gifted by the ARU. Due to a confidentiality clause in the contract that I signed, I can't and won't disclose the amount paid to each Wallaroo for that World Cup effort (nor to embarrass the ARU either). We were grateful for the contribution that was provided to us all. It was the beginning of something very new for women's rugby in Australia and it had to start somewhere.

I can honestly say that I feel blessed to have come into the rugby arena at the time that I did. Playing for money or contracts was not a "thing", we played for the love of the game, our mates and the green and gold. All of those things were an absolute privilege.

The finals of the World Cup were played on the 16th of May, 1998. New Zealand were the best side on ground and came out on top (as predicted before the tournament got underway). Those girls are amazing to watch and deserved to win. What a privilege it was to have been a part of the first ever World Cup where the Wallaroos were included and the event sanctioned by the IRB. We all enjoyed a closing dinner and the afterparty.

The amazing coaching staff and management for our first World Cup campaign included Head Coach Bob Hitchcock, Assistant Coach Shelley Lingman, Team Manager Joan Forno, and Assistant Manager Christine Gold. Our doctor was Kath Gaffney and physio Jenny Birckel. Our team (alphabetical order) included:

Libby Andrew, Holly Birch, Bronwyn Calvery, Karen Bucholz, Lisa-Jane Dwan, Louise Ferris, Mieke Gladwin, Bronwyn Hart, Christine Henson, Perise Illi, Bronwyn Laidlaw, Melissa Latu, Bronnie Mackintosh, Ronnie May, Sherilee Moulds, Sharon O'Kane, Tui Ormsby, Tanya Osborn, Pearl Palaialii, Naomi Roberts, Shirley Russell, Helen Theunissen, Rebecca Wakim, Nicole Wickert (captain) and Selena Worsley.

Amongst the World Cup souvenirs that I kept included our "Australian Women's Rugby Union Team" songbook. Of course it was Joan, our team manager who compiled the song book, perhaps because a portion of our team were not born in Australia and did not yet know the words to the following songs: Waltzing Matilda, Advance Australia Fair, We are the Champions, Run Wallaby Run, When a Hero Comes Along, Waltzing Matilda (Traditional), World in Union, Still Call Australia Home, Let Go and the band played Waltzing Matilda. The front page of the booklet included an extract of Nelson Mandela's inaugural speech from 1994. The words of this great man gave me the same goosebumps that the words of each song in our booklet did. It was a privilege to be in the team and to sing these songs together as we travelled on the bus to here and there, wandered home from training and in the pubs around the world. Precious memories. Thank you Joan for the book and this keepsake.

Post World Cup attendance I headed across to Africa with Sharrin and spent the following six weeks on the back of a Kumuka Overland Safari Truck. We wandered safely around the Masai Mara and Serengeti game parks, searching for and photographing the Big 5. We spotted and got close to all five plus loads more native animals that I had only ever seen in books. It was a blast. I loved the visit to Africa and the entire experience. I love Africa. The camping and gaming experience was topped off with our final week of holidays spent on a beach in Zanzibar. It was a brilliant end to a six-month training and playing stint of rugby, some of the most rewarding memories of my life. Unbeknownst to me at the time, the best was still yet to come.

After the break in Africa, Sharrin and I returned to Darwin, just in time for another annual National Women's Rugby Championship, this time played in my new hometown Darwin from the 12-19th July, 1998. I would play for the first time as a Northern Territory representative, coming up against my ACT teammates who I had to face when I played in the WA jersey in 1995. By the time this tournament came around, I had represented the ACT, WA and now NT at the same tournament. I certainly was collecting a huge collection of tracksuits and playing jerseys, all up to this point as #6 or #7, the position that I loved the most, on either side of the scrum, as the open or blindside flanker.

At the end of the 15s season in Darwin, I backed up for the Southern Comfort Club 10s on Friday, 18th of September, 1998 at Rugby Park, Marrara. There was no shortage of rugby this year for the women's game. Pints, Litchfield, Uni and South Darwin all had women's teams in the

WALLAROOS FIRST WORLD CUP 1998

local Darwin competition. I loved the challenge of 10s and the extra room it provided on the field. I loved to run, and used to cover about 7km in a 15-a-side match so God only knows how far I would run in a 10-a-side game.

After the 10s the annual Australia Day matches and sevens competitions in Darwin would come around. Australian and NZ players from both women's and men's sides would battle it out for the best team. The games were vicious, and I captained this Australian team in 1998 when we finally won something!

The Australia Day Sevens Tournament was played over the 23rd and 24th of January, 1999, and was again a fierce and fast competition with loads of tries and plenty of room for running.

The local Darwin competition finals were played in late March, 1999, and my first season in the top end came to an exhausting end. I was in my prime and ready for selection in the Aussie Gold Sevens Team to travel to Hong Kong for my second performance.

After the Darwin local comp was wrapped up and finals played, I had received news of my selection in the training squad of 30 women. Only 22 players would be chosen for the match against New Zealand on the 29th of August, 1999 (scheduled as a curtain raiser to the Bledisloe Cup Test at the Sydney Football Stadium).

The squad that I made assembled on the 26th of August, 1999, to prepare for this match. Most of this team had represented Australia at the recent World Cup, but up and coming players were constantly popping up and disappearing each season.

A letter from coach Bob Hitchcock followed on from the selection one mentioned above. Joan Forno was our team manager, and we were required to bring along our "number one" kit from the World Cup to the training camp and prep for Test Match. Numbers ones were our "formal and official uniform" while our number twos were our "tracksuits/playing/training gear". I look back now and laugh at the fact that we were having to bring back the uniforms previously worn to save money in the women's budget. Ah you have to love women's sport and the requests back in the 20th century. I am hoping the girls are not asked to do same 30 years on (or the men either).

The Wallaroos Squad who made the final cut for the Test Match above included 22 names from the World Cup team. New players to the Wallaroos included: Anita Carlin, Louise Cooke, Annita Flannery, Kristy Frogley, Sarah Gardiner, Debbie Grylls, Frances Lee and Kelly Sager (the squad had been cut back from 30).

My playing and training continued. The Northern Territory Institute of Sport offered me a scholarship to assist with my training which I gratefully accepted. Kym Thurbon, a Royals and ACT coach from my first year playing rugby (1992) turned up in Darwin with the same, if not more, enthusiasm than when I had first met this bloke in Canberra. Kym was an amazing coach, and I learned a lot from him. I really enjoyed his style of training and the manner which he still has today.

1998 World Cup Squad

A TRUCKLOAD OF 15S AND 7S RUGBY

Having arrived at the beginning of this chapter, you have already been on a short trip into the very first Australian Women's Development Squad and camp of 1993. Although we had already played in two annual tournaments in Newcastle, this was another new beginning for women's rugby in Australia. It felt like the initial warm up was done and now the ARU were testing the water to determine what type of talent was available.

I knew I wanted to be a part of that 1993 development team and it was a privilege to have been selected and present for that very first camp in Newcastle. The jersey I was given in that camp is one of my favourites and the memories of that weekend remain. Everything about that camp was fun, the girls were fun to be around, the staff were all great and, the physical demands of the camp were challenging. I was required to use my brain and concentrate on a range of new topics. I had never sat in a classroom before and talked about these the importance of training, playing and recovery. There was a lot for me to learn and a lot of new practices I needed to commence, and I was keen.

After sharing these details with you, I brought you along to the first international series when the New Zealand ladies visited Australia and walloped us, on three separate occasions in 1994. It still hurts to think back to those beatings. We were all so young and inexperienced, yet we were so full of enthusiasm it didn't really matter whether we won or lost. I feel humbled. We had to start somewhere in this new game for women and Sydney was the perfect location for our first ever international test. Besides, it was not only central for the majority of the Aussie team, but it was also a good location for the international flight to and from New Zealand. It was a thrill to have been a part of these firsts for Australian women's rugby.

In 1995 while I was having a break from playing sport and experiencing "paid employment" in Western Australia, the Wallaroos toured to NZ and played in the second Test Match, losing the Laurie O'Reilly Cup for the second time.

My aim in this chapter is to try, without boring you, to wrap up a truckload of club, representative, national and international women's rugby union. You can skip this chapter and the detail contained in it (and I won't be offended) or you can learn what the journey for women in my era playing rugby union entailed. It was a whole lot of fun and included loads of rugby.

1996

I returned home to Canberra on the feast of St Patrick's Day and left my role at the Immigration and Processing Centre in Port Hedland. My life, again, was about to change dramatically, as was the weather!

Annually in Canberra, the local rugby union tournament commenced after the annual Easter holidays. That means that from April, 1996, I was already back at rugby training and playing not only in a newly formed

A TRUCKLOAD OF 15S AND 7S RUGBY

Canberra competition for women (which was 10-per-side only), but also for our ACT representative team, which by then was called the Canberra Kestrels. I was playing in the Sydney Women's Rugby Union Competition for the Kestrel's in my favourite position as open side flanker. Effectively I was playing two games of women's rugby every weekend.

In June 1996, the Alberta Rugby Union Women's Team toured to Australia and played four games of women's 15-per-side rugby (in a period of two weeks). They played their first game against NSW on the 19th of June, 1996, before catching a bus to Canberra for the second ever visiting women's international game in the nation's capital. This was not an international Test Match given the ladies from Alberta were a provincial side only. It was all good experience for us Aussies and we felt excited to host visitors from another nation.

The Canberra game was played on Saturday, 22nd of June, 1996. The Alberta women next flew to Brisbane and played against Queensland women's rugby representative side on the 25th of June, 1996, before returning to Sydney for a game against Australia Presidents XV as a curtain-raiser before the men's Canadian team played the Wallabies on the 29th of June, 1996. This was an extraordinary quantity of 15-per-side rugby in this short period but it was the way the women rolled and took advantage of the opportunity to gain experience.

The Canberra game was played at Manuka Oval at 2pm. The team I played in was called the ACT Brumbies Women and included: Louise Cooke, Glenda Merritt, Gen Job, Amber Johnson, Kristy Butt, Christine Rogers, Vikki Fisher, Ronnie May, Louise Ferris, Margaret Brennan, Sharon O'Kane, Louise Barron, Cassandra Sutton, Karen Aldons, Kathy Flemming, Libby Andrew, Belinda Todd, Deanne Murray, Karen Wilcox, Matina Stanfield and Justine Buist. Our coach was Col Spence and we were managed by Fiona O'Brien and Sharrin Wells.

Our opposition from Alberta included: Rachel Becker, Katie Berghofer, Heather Denkhaus, Linda Evenson, Nicols Fairburn, Kim Finlay, Tannis Franks, Jessica Hokanson, Michelle Hunter, Susan Johnson, Rhonda Kuzio, Andrea Lover, June Low, Brenda McKenzie, Candance Mergle, Jo

Reinbold, Jamie Samual, Tracey Simpson, Kristen Todd, Lauren Wooley, Colleen Bowers, Meghan Jasper, Susan Paul, Anne Stephens-Nauman and Heidi Schoening. Their coach was John O'Hanley and they were managed by Marilyn Scott.

The tour from the Canadian ladies gave us Aussies some real hope that we might be competitive on the international women's rugby circuit. Our only opposition until this year had been the New Zealand ladies.

The Canadian ladies were a better match for our level of rugby experience and skill. Even though they had been playing women's rugby since the 1980s, their first international match was played against USA in 1987. Canada also participated in the very first Women's Rugby World Cup in 1991. Geographically, their nation is located a lot closer to the women's rugby action that was coming out of the US, Europe and the British Isles during this period of growth in our sport.

Following this tour in June, and in between weekends of the local ACT and NSW tournaments, our Canberra representative team would also line up for the Annual Australian Women's Rugby Union Championship held at Pittwater Rugby Park, Sydney from the 15-20th of July, 1996. There were two pools; Pool A had NSW, WA, SA and QLD while Pool B had VIC, ACT and NT. This tournament was the first occasion where each state and territory were represented by one representative team.

At the conclusion of this championship (which QLD won), the squad would be announced for a national squad camp, scheduled for August 1996. We already had a solid foundation for the Wallaroos to continue to build upon and new players were constantly arriving at the national tournament. The level of play and the standard of fitness were rising with each year and noticeably. The 1996 Schweppes Wallaroos were selected following the national championship and once again, I heard my name read aloud. I was excited.

The team gathered for a training camp in Sydney in preparation to play against the New Zealand Black Ferns. On the last day of August, 1996, the

A TRUCKLOAD OF 15S AND 7S RUGBY

Australian Schweppes Wallaroos played a third international test match against the New Zealand Women's Team. This match was played at Waratah Stadium, Concord at 2.30pm and there would have been barely 100 spectators in the grandstand. NZ won this third test 28-5, retaining the Laurie O'Reilly cup. The curtain raiser to this game was the Canberra Women's Kestrels versus Australian Defence Force Women's Academy (won by the Kestrels).

The 1996 rugby year was hectic and filled with a greater commitment from me to this sport than previously. I wanted a jersey in the World Cup Squad and that meant I would really have to up my level of fitness and skill if I was going to make the final cut.

This season's highlights included the international against Alberta, and the annual tournament in Sydney where we beat Victoria 55-0, Northern Territory 15-10 and lost to Queensland 30-5 in the Grand Final.

The NSW finals series saw our Canberra Kestrels Women's Team win the Jack Scott Cup. We won the semi against Drummoyne 31-0, though the Grand Final was a tougher contest between the same two teams, with us winning 17-6.

I had remained part of the original Royals women's team which won everything that was going, with local team Tuggeranong Vikings proving to be our toughest competition in Canberra. I decided at the end of that playing year I would break away from the Royals Club along with my partner Sharrin who was playing for Tuggeranong Vikings and start up a new team at the West Belconnen Rugby Club. The playing numbers were expanding, and another team would hopefully attract players from the Belconnen suburbs opposed to southern Canberra. I had the support and contacts from Wests so I thought it was a good opportunity to assist grow the sport a little more locally. There was nothing to lose and more rugby mates to be found.

To top off an amazing "comeback year" to the sport of women's rugby union, I was selected as one of three women to participate in a full membership with the ACT Academy of Sport. This scholarship was established to provide identified women's players with access to high performance coaching and technical expertise. Andy Clark became another coach in my life, and I had access to feedback and sessions with coaches like Scott Wisemantel and, of course, the great Bob Hitchcock, who became a long-time coach and friend.

This year was full. The advent of the local Canberra competition was one of the best things that happened for women's rugby in the capital city. This was progress. None of it would have been possible without the commitment of the army of volunteers, women and men who loved rugby and saw the vision that is enjoyed today. Huge thanks goes to Joanne Faulks and Genevieve Job who both held the position as president of our ACT women's rugby committee in these early years of the women's game in Canberra. Thanks also goes to our amazing coach Col Spence and sponsors Lannie and Pete Pomazak. Without these people, we would not have had a team on the paddock. Fiona O'Brien, Sharrin Wells, Bob Shakespeare, Matt Rainey, Anne Gallagher and Rinny were all heavily involved in various capacities in this amazing year for women's rugby in the ACT. Huge thanks also goes to our families and friends who continued to encourage and support us all. The local rugby clubs were accepting of the women's teams and also made us feel more and more a real part of the club (which was beginning to lose the "boys club" feel as more and more girls, colour and laughter entered the scene).

By the end of the 1996 rugby year, I should have been exhausted, but I was feeling the opposite. My journey with women's rugby was just heating up, and where the energy came to keep on moving forward with this sport came from is beyond me.

1997

In March 1997 I toured to Hong Kong for the very first international women's rugby sevens tournament. This was the commencement of a very busy rugby year for me personally and for the development of women's rugby in both 7s and 15s in Australia.

A TRUCKLOAD OF 15S AND 7S RUGBY

The 1997 Jack Scott Cup (Sydney women's weekend 15s competition) would include teams from: Warringah, Drummoyne, Wollongong University, Eastwood, Sydney University, Eastern Suburb, University of NSW and of course Canberra (we were still called Canberra Kestrels). The trusty old Royals bus would travel to Sydney most weekends to play against these teams. Warringah and Drummoyne were the toughest competition for our ACT side (who were victorious three years running). The NSW women's committee would distribute a monthly newsletter with results of each round game, the competition table and committee news. I express heartfelt thanks to the Sydney ladies and NSWRU who kept this competition going for us all to enjoy. The competition was building from strength to strength.

During May 1997, I participated in the Australian Women's Rugby Squad Camp, held in Brisbane. This was good preparation for yet another Test Match, this time against the visiting USA women's team (Eagles). The USA ladies hold the record as winners of the very first Women's Rugby World Cup 1991, they also came second place in the subsequent World Cups of 1994 and 1998.

The ACT Women played the USA Women on Tuesday, 22nd of July, 1997, at 7.00pm at the West Belconnen Leagues Club. Our team included: Louise Cooke, Sharrin Wells, Fran Lee, Kristy Butt, Gen Job, Penny Anderson, Libby Andrew, Christine Rogers, Louise Ferris, Alena Summers, Sharon O'Kane, Cassandra Sutton, Louise Barron, Renee Goninan, Deanne Murray, Jodie Bidjorac, Lindsay Morgan, Angel Shakespeare, Glenda Hyde, Melanie Bond, Kathy Flemming and Lids Hill. Coach was Col Spence, assistants were Orini Madrica and Bob Shakespeare, manager was Fiona O'Brien and physio was Di Howell.

USA Women: Meredith Ottens, Stacy Boyle, Mary Jane Soreson, Jennifer Sikora, Nancy Fitz, Diane Schnap, Erina Queen, Barbara Bond, Terese Taylor, Jos Bergmann, Joy Morrison, Amy Westerman, Katherine Borek, Justine Sleazer, Jen Crawford, Kimberly Cyganik, Liz Kerk, Jennifer Renne, Kalie Kim, Carol Burdick and Shalanda Baker. Coach was Frank Boivert and assistant was Joe Kelly.

This same USA women's team played against representative women's sides in Sydney and Brisbane before an International Test Match against our Australian Women. This test was played as a curtain raiser to the Australia vs South Africa men's Test Match on the 2nd of August, 1997, at Suncorp Stadium, Brisbane. USA won that game 28-24 which was not a bad effort from us Aussies.

The 1997 Squad Camp was held from the 12-14th of December in Mona Vale, Sydney. The main aim of this camp was to provide players with an opportunity to participate in education and workshop sessions designed to widen our understanding of the game and preparation necessary to improve our skills. It was also good fun and another chance for the team to get to know each other better prior to entering into the World Cup year.

1998

This year would be my first full season playing for South Darwin Women's Rugby Team. The local competition kicks off in October and runs through until March the following year. South Darwin was a great club and the team was filled with some amazing talent. Great friends were made. The consistent factor in each of the states in this country in which I played was that, even though the opposition on the field were the enemy, off the field they became mates. It is a huge aspect of the culture of rugby. The women's rugby competitions were all relatively small so when we arrived at playing for state level, so we became teammates with the opposition. This was a similar experience at the state and national level too. The girls from QLD and NSW who were considered arch enemies became really good friends. Therein lies one of the greatest gifts of playing rugby – the friendships.

1999

At the age of 28, I was backing up for my second tour to Hong Kong (March, 1999). It was nine months after the World Cup in Holland and I had played a lot of rugby in the Northern Territory in between these two commitments. I was fighting fit and hungry for another international meet.

I love sevens rugby, it's a wonderful challenging game with so much more space to run and plenty of room on the field to spread the ball. I found the game of 7s very different to 15s and I couldn't choose which one I preferred as I loved them both. Maybe I was better suited to 7s than 15s, I don't know, but on the occasions when I was selected in the national sides I responded and took the whole experience seriously.

It's always been odd to consider that the rugby programs in which I participated (during my time away from my workplaces) were considered for elite athletes. I never considered myself elite in any respect, and still do not. This is probably due to the fact that I had to work full time to be fully self-supporting (something that is important to me and my independence). I assume someone who is a "real elite athlete", would be in full time training, competing and travelling for a pay cheque as opposed to my experience.

I do feel grateful that being a real elite athlete was never my journey and that I had the privilege of being one of the trailblazers of this sport for women in Australia. Playing the game or training and travelling to be paid by the ARU would have made my experience and all those years a very different experience (and not my journey). I trained hard and played women's rugby because I loved the game. I loved training, I loved pushing myself and seeing the results that I achieved, but most of all I loved the fun that I had with my rugby mates. Rugby taught me a lot and brought people and experiences into my life that can never be taken away. No amount of money could ever be equal to those memories nor mates.

An invitation to trial for the NT police came unexpectedly from a few girls in my touch footy team. Darwin is a relatively small town and I had nothing to lose by attending the trial even though I probably had never really given a career in the police service a serious thought. My intention to attend the trial was simply to see if I might win a race or trophy. I never would have anticipated that event expanding into the additional ten years of my life (but that's a whole and another amazing story filled with as much fun and adventure as this rugby decade).

In 1999, I was still pretty quick off the ground (5.94 sec 40-metre sprint), super fit (% of V max 55), and strong (PB bench press 82.5kg). My body weight hovered about 70kg and beep test result at best was level 12 / 4. The staff at the Northern Territory Institute of Sport, throughout my entire playing career in the NT, were an amazing support to my fitness, skills and rugby, in every way. I undertook routine testing which regularly included my anthropometry, acceleration and speed, fitness, flexibility, strength and endurance and agility. I still have all my results and records from these years of my life including my daily training diary which I religiously completed.

On Wednesday, the 23rd of March, 1999, I departed Darwin, along with teammates Naomi Roberts and Mel Goher bound for Hong Kong. Our coach this year was Shelley Lingman (her first gig coaching the sevens team) and our physio was Stephanie Best. We were a total of five NT members of the 1999 Aussie Gold Sevens Team travelling from the top end and on the same flight. We overnighted in Kuala Lumpur before arriving in Hong Kong the following day.

Our host was an English guy called Tom. He met us at the airport and escorted us by bus to our accommodation, "The Empire", which was a very flash hotel. Our team dribbled into Honk Kong throughout that day, and we all waited for Joan to arrive and start organising us once again. We had a couple of free hours that afternoon to wander around the local area and shake off any effects from the flight.

Joan Forno's husband, Allan, accompanied our team to Hong Kong for this tour. We all loved Allan and the time with him provided us all with a chance to get to know him. Those Fornos are wonderful people and committed to Australian rugby 100%. They were like a surrogate pair of parents to us all.

This was the year I was selected as vice-captain of the Aussie Gold team. This meant extra meetings with the coach to go through game plans, team lists, and a few extra responsibilities. Our team was looking good, and we were gelling together nicely.

The 1999 Aussie Gold team included: Queenslanders: Deena Aitken, Karen Bucholz, Marie-Anne Kearney, Bronwyn Laidlaw and Tanya Osborn. NT players: Melanie Goher, Naomi Roberts and Libby Andrew. NSW: Rachel Hill and ACT: Sharon O'Kane. Coach: Shelley Lingman, Manager: Joan Forno and Physio: Stephanie Best.

The tournament kicked off on Friday, the 26th of March, 1999 at the Hong Kong Football Club. 12 teams would compete. Many of the original countries who competed in 1997 had returned including Hong Kong, Arabian Gulf, Aussie Gold, England Stormers, Fiji, Japan, New Zealand Wild Ducks, Singapore and USA. Participating for the first time in 1999 were China, Samoa and Russia. The teams were divided into four pools, with three teams in each.

The pools were as follows. Pool A: NZ Wild Ducks, Russia and Japan. Pool B: Aussie Gold, Hong Kong and Samoa. Pool C: USA, Fiji and China (late withdrawal from Fiji saw only 2 teams in C). Pool D: England Stormers, Singapore and Arabian Gulf.

Our first game on Friday, the 26th of March, 1999, was at 8:50am against Hong Kong and resulted in our first win 38-0. Our second game was against Samoa which we won 17-14 after a tough battle and a beautiful try by our winger Naomi Roberts (thank God!).

Our semifinal was played against the NZ "Wild Ducks". Those bloody Kiwis gave us a hiding again! We were defeated 38-0 by the better team and couldn't even get close to scoring once!

Our final game for the tournament was played against the English ladies in the playoff for third and fourth position. We won the game 12-10. I was pleased with the result which was an improvement from 5th place in 1997 but to be honest, day 2 of our tournament was tough and disappointing. I felt knackered. I can hear my dear old mum saying "Lib it's only football" but when you train for that long and hard, it was still disappointing.

WALLAROO #19

We had played only four games during this tournament, but the speed and intensity was high, and I had remained on the field for the entire duration of every game. Third in the world wasn't a bad effort at the end of this tournament. I was happy with the result and grateful for the opportunity to represent Aussie Gold again. I was learning more about the sevens game and loving it more and more too.

The women's final would be played on the ground where I had experienced that privilege two years before. The battle between the Kiwis and the USA ladies was fierce. The halves were ten minutes each way and this was the highest level of any women's rugby sevens that I had witnessed in my life.

The Kiwis, as expected, came out winners 29-0 and the game was a magnificent showcase of women's rugby sevens.

One of our teammates, Rachel, from NSW was celebrating her 21st birthday that evening. We all shared a few quiet drinks at the hotel bar, and the Poms, Arabs, Yanks and Kiwis were all there too. About midnight we all headed off to the local nightclub called Joe Banana's where the celebrations continued into the early hours of the following morning.

That year, 1999, I switched my Aussie Gold playing jersey with the #6 from the USA team. I still have her American jersey, along with the stars and stripes, hanging in my cupboard, all these years later. It has been a great gardening jersey.

It is common practice (or it was in my day) at the end of a major tournament for players to swap playing and or training kit. Some players would swap jumpers with their opposite numbers and other players preferred to keep their jersey in their own collection. I remember at my first World Cup there was a room provided in the hotel for a "jersey swapping session". Girls from countries across the world came prepared to swap all kinds of playing and training kit. It was great. One of my favourite swaps which remain in my treasure chest is a pair of Canadian women's rugby socks. These are red with a white band around the top of the leg and multi-coloured rainbow maple leaves around the top of the sock.

A TRUCKLOAD OF 15S AND 7S RUGBY

Prior to commencing my police training (5th of July, 1999), Sharrin and I skipped home to Canberra for a short break and to catch up with family. I, kind of accidently, unexpectedly (whoops Joan), fell onto the old familiar rugby league field and found myself playing in the annual national tournament. By the end of the final game, I had been selected for the Australian Women's Rugby League Team (the Jillaroos)!

The annual Women's Rugby League National Championships just so happened to coincide with this trip on the June long weekend (the same weekend I had previously travelled to Newcastle in 1992, 1993 and 1994 to play union). We could not resist going along to support the Canberra ladies' team, especially given my background in the local Canberra team and my love for this game too. Besides, I was on a short holiday and enjoying some time off.

West Belconnen Rugby League Complex hosted this tournament, which by now was in its 5th year. From little things, big things were growing right before my eyes. I recall the atmosphere at the familiar playing ground and upon arriving to spectate was excited to see how the game had grown. The standard of play had increased significantly too and it was exciting (although always hard to watch and not play).

It wasn't long after discovering that the ACT team were low on numbers (due to injuries), that I found myself borrowing a pair of boots and running onto the field half-dressed and hungry for some action. I didn't even have a mouth guard, but I was too excited to even care. Someone had told me I could play, and I could not resist the chance to get out onto that field and get my hands on that ball. It had been more than six years since my last game of rugby league, and I ran amok. I thoroughly enjoyed playing with the ACT girls. Believe it or not, some of the originals (Cath, Bushy, Leeanne and Squiz) from 1991 were still present, in coaching and support roles and spectating in the grandstand.

I never told Joan nor Bob Hitchcock about my selection and the offer from the Australian Women's Rugby League. Although it would have been fun and exciting to become a dual international, I felt it would be unfair of me to accept that offer. Let's call it a privilege. Sharrin and I kept very quiet for fear of getting in trouble from Joan and the ARU. Thank God I was not injured, nor prevented from starting my basic police training in Darwin. I did have loads of fun that weekend and enjoyed a great catch up with the Canberra legends but I will admit it was risky and naughty. I still love league, absolutely love the hooker's role in the #9 jersey where all the action is found (on the field I am referring to)! These games in Canberra were the last few games of footy I would play for this calendar year. It was a great ending and I felt happy.

The annual Women's Rugby Union Championship in 1999 was hosted by Perth, Western Australia. The dates, 4th-10th July, clashed with my first week of training in the police college Berrimah, so for the first time in eight years, something took priority over my rugby. I made the decision with ease, I was ready for a new challenge and this new ball game called policing felt exciting. Sharrin headed off as assistant coach of the NT women's side, along with coach Kym Thurbon for some fun at the nationals.

For the next ten weeks I put my head into the law books and challenged my brain matter in a way I don't think I had ever cared to before 1999. I was loving the challenge of the college, the physical training, defensive tactics, driver training and every other skills that I would learn during my training. After six months in the college and not one day off, I graduated with yet another trophy, this one not for scoring tries but as the most outstanding recruit overall Squad 66/99. I was shocked to be the recipient of this award and like most of those occasions, I felt embarrassed to be singled out especially during the graduation ceremony where I had to march and salute on my lonesome and in front of the squad and crowd. Commissioner Brian Bates was the boss in those days and my life and daily duties were about to change, and dramatically.

2000

The 1st of January the following year was the turn of the century, and all cops in Alice Springs were on deck for the anticipated midnight antics

A TRUCKLOAD OF 15S AND 7S RUGBY

(my first operational shift of 20 hours had been Christmas Eve)! The year 2000 was shaping up to be exciting in both work and play. Sharrin and I were building our first house together in Diarama Close, Alice Springs and it was also the year that Sydney hosted the Olympic Games.

Thinking back to that year, there is no way I ever dreamed that women would be playing rugby sevens at the Olympics, I mean ever! Yet look what happened from this beginning of the women's rugby sevens game in 1997. The Australian Women's Sevens Team were not only represented, wearing green and gold uniforms at the 2016 Rio Summer Olympics, but were gold medal winners. What a thrill for those girls (permitted to be called Australia) and proudly representing our entire nation. I wonder if they even knew how the women's tournaments started and the journey we had all travelled prior to their entry into such an amazing opportunity. It still blows my mind that women are actually playing rugby sevens on the Olympic stage. We have come so far and are doing so well, finally after all those early years of battles, judgements, underfunding, the list goes on. It is truly rewarding to sit back and have the privilege of watching this amazing game on TV!

Congratulations to coach Tim Walsh and players: Emilee Cherry, Ellia Green, Nicole Beck, Shannon Parry, Emma Tonegato, Sharni Williams, Evania Pelite, Gemma Etheridge, Charlotte Caslick, Chloe Dalton, Alicia Quirk and Amy Turner. What an amazing achievement for everyone who made this possible and for our nation. I felt proud of the girls (and annoyed that I was too old to make the team nor invited to even trial given I would have turned up)! I am wishing the Aussie women's sevens rugby girls the best of luck in the upcoming Olympics in Paris, France (as this book goes to print in July 2024 and I continue to feel jealous that I am now too old and slow to play).

On the 29th of June, 2000, day 22 of the 2000 Summer Olympics Torch Relay, I had the privilege of running with the Olympic torch along a main street in Darwin. I had been selected as one of the 11,000 Australians who had this pleasure and thrill. This was due to my rugby playing career (and like that feeling on the HK rugby field and at my police graduation ceremony, I felt embarrassed and awkward with so many people looking at me). To be honest, I ran as bloody fast as I could with that torch and handed the flame over to the next runner in world record time. It honestly was an honour that day to be involved, to get to keep the torch and uniform (and add these to my chest of rugby treasures)! These are framed and hang in our home along with the Queen's Baton, Commonwealth Games Torch Relay of 2006 (Alice Springs). That was another privilege I experienced due to my rugby representation and efforts. I ran up Anzac Hill, escorted by a couple of local cops, to pass the baton's flame to the next runner and soak up the experience in yet another new hometown. I loved Alice Springs and loved the years I spent living there too.

The Hong Kong Women's Rugby Sevens and Inaugural Asian Championship 2000 was held on Thursday, 23rd of March at the Happy Valley Sportsground and Friday, 24th of March at Hong Kong Football Club.

The teams this year included 12 of the finest women's rugby sevens teams from around the world at that stage of the development of this game. NZ Wild Ducks were the champs and had returned to HK for some more action, along with runners-up from 1999, the USA.

Aussie Gold, Samoa, Wales and the Netherlands were all returning for another taste of HK Sevens and to try and knock NZ off their winning streak. I said TRY. The 2000 tournament saw the influx of some brand-new talent to the arena including Japan, Singapore, Thailand, Arabian Gulf, Kazakhstan and of course the Hong Kong ladies (who hopefully had forgotten about that exhibition match of 1997 on the main stadium, a game I would never ever forget and still remains probably one of my all-time favourites).

The two pools were as follows. Pool A: New Zealand Wild Ducks, Samoa, Wales, Hong Kong, Thailand, and the Arabian Gulf. Pool B: United States, Australia (whoops who wrote that in the program – we were registered as Aussie Gold), Netherlands, Japan, Kazakhstan and Singapore.

A TRUCKLOAD OF 15S AND 7S RUGBY

Our Aussie team included: Elizabeth Andrew (ACT), Karen Bucholz (QLD), Debbie Grylls (QLD), Bronwyn Laidlaw (QLD), Bronnie Mackintosh (NSW), Tanya Osborne (QLD), Sharon O'Kane (ACT), Tui Ormsby (NSW), Naomi Roberts (NT) and Cheryl Soon (NSW).

Team colours: gold jersey with navy collar and embroidery, navy rugby shorts, gold and navy socks (thanks to Joan Forno who again organised this for the team). Coach: Bob Hitchcock and assistant: Shelley Lingman. Manager: Joan Forno, physio: Stephanie Best.

Hong Kong Rugby Sevens

A TRUCKLOAD OF 15S AND 7S RUGBY

Our 2000 7s team was made up entirely from a group of 15s players located somewhere across our nation (NSW, NT, QLD, ACT and WA). 15s in this year was still in its infancy in Australia and the numbers of females playing the sport was rising each year as was the standard.

Flying into Hong Kong to compete in these tournaments were the first occasions that the Aussie Gold players would meet and get to know each other. Not only were we usually from opposing teams, but we had also never trained nor played together (for the majority and given there were only ten positions up for grabs). The distances in between our hometowns and local rugby clubs rendered the cost too great for our limited budget but we made the most of each opportunity.

Sharon O'Kane (ACT), Tanya Osborn (QLD) and I (from all over, ACT, WA and NT) were the only survivors from the previous two tours to Hong Kong. As you will have come to expect by now, I have the results of every match played that year. To save you from getting bored with rugby stats: I can report that the "Bowl Championship" was played off between Singapore and Japan. Japan won and took home the bowl from their first ever appearance. I still remember how happy and excited that team were.

The "Plate Championship" was battled out between the Netherlands and Kazakhstan. Kazakhstan, again newcomers to the Honkers arena, came out on top and won that final.

The "Cup Championship", the main event, was played between Aussie Gold and the Wild Ducks, two nations who battle everything and fiercely (and both sides unsupported by the home unions and needing to play under their pseudo team names). Those bloody Kiwis were too good for us on the day! New Zealand Wild Ducks would take that Cup home AGAIN, for the third time in this early history of women's sevens. Our opposition was outstanding and as frustrated as I still feel, they deserved the cup. We were no match for their skill, speed and talent ... yet.

WALLAROO #19

The inaugural Asian Championship Cup final was won by Kazakhstan. I have little to share with you about this team except two things; we were unexpectedly surprised that they gave us a "run for our money".

To briefly summarise our result in 2000:

We played Kazakhstan in our first game and won 12-7. Next up was Japan who were feisty and fit but didn't have the rugby experience. We managed a good 29-5 win once we found our rhythm. The next game was a draw with the USA ladies 7-7 and a great, tough, battle which we just could not win. The Netherlands were our next victims whom we beat 45-7.

Feedback from Bob in one of the many letters he wrote to me: "gives wholeheartedly all the time, both on and off the field. She played in every game of the tournament and her fitness is a tribute to the work that she is obviously doing". What was even more remarkable was that I had maintained my position on this team when I thought I would have been wiped off the team list due to my move to Alice Springs for work and the fact I was living in the middle of the Australian desert without any women's competition for a minimum of about 2,000 kms away.

My ability to maintain a position within this team and a few yet to come is with thanks to the NTIS who funded my "elite athlete scholarship". This scholarship provided me with funding to travel back and forward to Sydney every two-three weeks during the 2001 Sydney Women's Rugby Competition. I played on and off for the West Harbour ladies' team and also represented NSW during this year (huge thanks to my great mate Loui Ferris and the team for making a space for me) which wasn't a bad effort for a probationary constable working long shifts on a rotating roster. Although at this time my work at the police station was starting to take priority over my training, I didn't have a good reason to retire from this sport. I was loving the challenge at work, and I started to rely on my rugby playing and training experience, not so much the fitness training that was started to take a back seat.

A TRUCKLOAD OF 15S AND 7S RUGBY

My work role at the local police station exploded into a whole new world for me where I wandered into other people's trauma and tragedies most days. There were suicides, fatal traffic crashes, domestic violence incidents, and a range of other new experiences that I had prepared for (as much as one can) in the preceding six months in the training college. But nothing could have prepared me for general duties in the Alice. I was absolutely loving the challenge of my new role and well suited to this profession especially given my adult child characteristics.

My first shift in Alice Springs was Christmas Eve and Sgt Lorraine Carlon politely advised us that the shift would be 20 hrs. It was an unexpected welcome to policing. I thank God for Lorraine and the other staff who guided me through those first 18 months of my probationary period as a young recruit. Mick Bourke was my first senior partner, and Stewie Baum my second. I was supported and taught by some great cops, men and women all very committed to their service in uniform. I was on a very steep learning curve. I noticed the public rarely called to just share some good news! I was and have always been attracted to trauma (in those days while I was young and energetic anyway). So when I wasn't at work or miles out of town attending to a crash or visiting a remote community, I was training for my next rugby match either in Sydney, Hong Kong or Europe.

My trusty pushy took me everywhere I needed to go while living in the Alice. Palm Circuit was my first home and a quick ride through the gap to the local police station on Bath Street. I did my weight training and skills work (sometimes fitness in the air conditioning) at the local YMCA. The only female superintendent in the NT at the time, from the Investigations Unit, Kate Vanderlaan was a very keen gym goer and a regular at the YMCA too. Before long, Kate and I became gym buddies, sharing weight training programs and serious gains. I was lucky to have found not only a dedicated weight training partner in Kate but a friend and mentor too. Kate went further than most females within the ranks of the NT police force. She was a great role model for many of us, not just females. Kate was the very first female cop, Australia-wide to ride a police motorbike (possibly to trade in those horrendous police dresses and handbags of that era in the Northern Territory)!

The year 2000 was a big one for me. I knew I was becoming more dedicated and interested in my ever-changing role at the police station, yet I remained hungry for selection. The English Women's Team were coming to Australia for a tour during May 2001 and I was interested to see if I could maintain a position on the team. Of course, the 2002 World Cup was also on the horizon, but I was starting to favour my work role than the training paddock, which was getting further and further away. I was teamless in Alice and from time to time I would join the Alice Springs Dingoes (men's police rugby team) for training if it fit into my roster. I trained on regardless. If I wasn't at work and working overtime, I was at training or asleep! To my excitement and joy, I received the invite to Hong Kong. This would be my fourth and final tour (I promise).

2001

Looking back through my rugby file of 2001, I see a noticeable change. This file is a thick one, another busy year with representative rugby. I kept everything from this year (like the previous ones) including the old boarding passes which were a thing before mobile phones and online check in. I notice this year there are documents that didn't exist prior to 2001. There is change, everything feels more professional and improved.

This year we received a spiral bound "2001 Hong Kong 7's Aussie Gold Players Manual". I assume it was either Joan Forno or coach Geoff Threlfo that compiled this document for the team. This was new and a clear step up in my fourth tour.

The Aussie Gold 2001 included: Elizabeth Andrew (NT), Debbie Grylls (QLD), Lisa Fiaola (NSW), Louise Ferris (NSW), Alexandra Hargreaves (NSW), Bronwyn Mackintosh (NSW), Tui Ormsby (WA), Naomi Roberts (NT), Charmain Smith (NSW) and Cheryl Soon (WA). Coach: Geoff Threlfo, Manager: Joan Forno and Physiotherapist: David Bayldon.

The tournament was held from Thursday, 29th of March – Friday, 30th March, 2001, and the title had also undergone a makeover: Women's

A TRUCKLOAD OF 15S AND 7S RUGBY

Rugby Sevens and Asian Championship 2001. It was held at So Kon Po Recreation Ground, Causeway Bay, Hong Kong.

The one consistent thing about my rugby file for 2001 was the handwritten diary which I kept and wrote in each day of the tour. "Here I am sitting on the flight waiting to take off to Hong Kong for the very last time. Sharrin is sitting to my left and these planes aren't built for comfort!"

The diary entries take me back and reminds me of the good friends and people who supported Sharrin and I during this period of our lives and my rugby career. Brad Quiggen had given us a ride to the airport and friends Sonya and Jenny had come to wave us off.

One part of this year's diary entry which I am willing to share here, is another visit to see my family. Given we were departing for Honkers from the East Coast and so close to Canberra it warranted a visit to see my parents and the growing number of nieces and nephews in the next generation of my family (my parents have a total of 24 grandchildren).

Mum was sitting up in the loungeroom when we arrived home. Nothing much changes at Renmark Street. The two TVs were blaring, Mum was sitting in her lounge chair listening to a game of rugby league on her tranny whilst watching two different games of whatever sport was available and knitting all at the same time. We sat up for a while catching up and talking during the ad breaks. I headed to bed in the bedroom from my childhood, hoping to dream of footy and scoring tries, the chip-chase-re-gather and score, all night.

This final year at Hong Kong, we stayed in yet another accommodation, this time the Island Pacific Hotel on Connaught Road West. My roomie for this tour was Lisa (otherwise known as Barbs). Barbs resembled a real-life barbie doll except she was, in addition to her good looks, an amazingly talented rugby player. She was fast, tough and I was glad she was on my team that's for sure.

By the 27th of March the ten of us and management team had arrived at the hotel. We were straight into meeting and organising the tour, and the flash new manual proved very helpful, containing all the information that we all needed.

The following day we trained. This was the only period spent together as a team before game day. There was never much time to get familiar with each other, either on or off the field but we did the best with what we were afforded (even though this was not ideal prep) and possibly one of the reasons why we just had not yet beaten those bloody Kiwis (who had been in HK for a whole week before we even arrived). This was women's rugby sevens 2001 Australian style and we were grateful for every moment.

Like all other years, we had morning and afternoon training. This ended with a pool session before the cocktail party hosted by the Hong Kong Rugby Union. It was a lovely get together, but no one was interested in a single cocktail, just wishing that tomorrow would come quick, and we could get our hands on that Gilbert.

Our team was registered under the banner of Aussie Gold, yet by this stage Hong Kong were calling us Australia (which I am not sure the ARU would have been happy about). Nonetheless the teams which landed in Pool B included: Australia, USA, England, Netherlands, Hong Kong, Thailand and Singapore. Pool A included: New Zealand, Samoa, Sweden, Kazakhstan, China, Japan and the Arabian Gulf.

Thursday morning on the 29th of March, 2001, finally arrived and our first game was 9:50am against Hong Kong. Every time I hear the women's team's name "Hong Kong" my mind takes me to the big stadium in 1997 and the experience playing that women's team on the main ground comes flooding back. It makes me smile and then I feel confident given I have played these ladies previously.

But this was 2001 and I was focused. Besides, this was the last time I would ever get to match up against our host nation. We had a comfortable win, 43-0. Our team came together on the field and Geoff, like all three previous coaches, did a great job guiding us all throughout the tournament.

A TRUCKLOAD OF 15S AND 7S RUGBY

Our 2nd match was at 12:50pm against the Netherlands and we had another enjoyable win, this time 45-0. By this time we had executed all of the set plays from our new flashy manual and were feeling confident going into the next and final game of the day. Our goal was to win every game, and we would need to if we were to make the Grand Final.

Our final match was played at 3:30pm against England. We were defeated 27-0 by a team which included: Teresa Andrews, Nicky Crawford, Emily Feltham, Nicki Jupp, Eilidh Smith, Susie Appleby, Lizzie Cribbs, Emma Mitchell, Jenny Phillips and Jo Yapp (coach was Rob Drinkwater). Some but not all of these girls had become familiar faces to me over the years of visiting Honkers and playing in this same tournament. The great thing about rugby is that, post the business end of games, there are usually a few lemonades to be shared at the bar.

These girls and they way they played in this match, destroyed my dream of getting to the Grand Final of my last Hong Kong Sevens tour. I could only play my best on the day and comfortably say that this team were in a league above our standard in Australia at this time.

The other great thing about rugby is, later this same year we would meet up again in a test series (15 per side not 7s) mid-year. So there would be an opportunity for some payback (if you could catch the buggers)!

On Friday, 30th of March, 2001 our first game was 11:00am against USA. Sadly, we lost to another better and more experienced team, with a final score of 17-0. This game, this tournament helped me to learn that if Aussie Gold was ever going to really compete seriously, we needed more preparation time pre-tournament together and had a long way to go if we were ever going to win.

The USA girls that beat our team for my final appearance included: Anita Pease, Diane Schnapp, Kerri McCabe, Erina Queen, Lisa Rowe, Krista McFarren, Emilia Jouycs, Laura Cabrera, Yancy Graf, Pam Irby and coach Emilio Signes. They were good but they were not unbeatable. They had more experience than us (and possibly had arrived a day or two before we did). We hadn't done too badly. Nonetheless I felt disappointed – I wanted to win.

The rest of the tournament was simply an opportunity for me to enjoy my last sevens games in Hong Kong. Our next match was against Sweden which we comfortably won 31-0. It was great to have a match against a Scandinavian country which was a first for me and our team.

This win left us with the opportunity to come home with that bloody plate (not the cup) again, but any plate is a good plate and better than no plate and a good reward for the huge effort of the Aussie Gold players, management and coaching staff too.

Our last game and my final game of international sevens rugby was played at 3:10pm against the Kazakhstan National Team. We won the match 41-12, then it was party time.

That same evening, the final of the women's sevens was played at the Hong Kong Stadium between New Zealand and USA. The match was amazing, the girls did all of us proud and guess what? Those Kiwis defeated the yanks 22-10 (and I knew the pain that those American girls were feeling)! Well done New Zealand.

We celebrated with a formal dinner at the Hong Kong Football Club and enjoyed the afterparty well into the early hours of the following day. Sharrin was there to celebrate with me for this final time and I was ready to call it a day. Cheers Hong Kong and to every female player that gave me a run for my money, to my Aussie Gold teammates and coaches and Joan. Thank you, what a privilege it had been to return four times to an amazing and developing space for women's rugby sevens. I know from my own experience that those years would not have been possible either, without the effort of the local women's committee, the Hong Kong RFU and the support of so many un-named volunteers. I remain grateful to you all.

By the end of this tour there was another noticeable change coming into our women's game. It was the increase of female referees, and I am talking worldwide. Alongside my teammates, I witnessed an amazingly talented and brave Aussie referee, Carolyn Tutty (nee Warren).

Carolyn was present at Hong Kong, running faster than me down the sideline and blowing that annoying whistle of hers (and not taking any crap from any player)! Carloyn was active in the whites for my entire rugby journey. I believe she first started blowing the whistle in 1991.

Carolyn officiated at the Women's Rugby Championships in 1994, 1995 and 1998. She was a touch judge during our inaugural Test Match against the Kiwis in 1994 Sydney and was also running about with that whistle at our Women's Rugby World Cup 1998 in Holland.

Carolyn, I just wanted to shine a spotlight on your service to not only the women's game but your support and love for rugby. You are one of the champions who made our sport great and allowed it to progress (and maybe entice other girls to pick up a whistle too). It cannot be an easy role you play, and I know you aren't in it for the huge pay cheque like the rest of us. You were an inspiration. Thank you for being a part of my rugby experience, thank you from us all worldwide for your refereeing service. I often felt proud of you when I saw you officiating a game between two international countries. I continually heard your Aussie accent loud and clear and in full control of the game. You are a credit to yourself, the referees' community, Australia and the game of women's rugby. Thanks again.

Aussie Gold Team touring Hong Kong

A TRUCKLOAD OF 15S AND 7S RUGBY

In summary of my Honkers tours:

Those Kiwis won the cup EVERY SINGLE YEAR! During the first year, Wild Ducks beat USA in the final 43-0. 1999 was the same, though the margin was a little less with the final score reading 29-0. In the year 2000 we finally made the cup final and were defeated by NZ 36-10 (at least we scored)! Which meant we touched the ball too, an improvement on previous years' play. In my final tour NZ would beat USA again 22-10. My hat goes off to every single player of the NZ women's teams' during my time, including:

1997: Monique Hiroranaa, Louisa Wall, Dianne Apiti, Ria Aetira, Suzy Shortland, Tasha Williams, Sharleen Holden, Annaleah Rush, Matta Young, Anna Richards and coach Darryl Suasua.

1998: No tournament due to this being the World Cup year for women.

1999: Annaleah Rush, Melodie Robinson, Monique Hirovanna, Sharleen Holden, Suzy Shortland, Kellie Kiwi, Hannah Myers, Dianne Kahura, Tammi Wilson, Winafred Kupa and Coach Darryl Suasu.

2000: This was the first year that I would witness the New Zealand ladies wearing their cherished black jersey. They were now officially called the Black Ferns. Full credit to the NZRU who stepped up to the plate and recognised the talent of these women and realised they were worth the investment. Laurie O'Reilly would be smiling that's for sure. Adidas had provided their full playing kit and these girls looked and played like professionals.

The team this year was: Annaleah Rush, Sharleen Holden, Monique Hirovanaa, Dianne Kahura, Tammi Wilson, Lavina Gould, Hannah Myers, Melodie Robinson, Anna Richards, Noi Kurei, Karangi Jones, Cecily Stainton, Sherry Hansen, Exia Shelford, Suzy Shortland, Stephanie Mortimer, Jody Darley and Coach Darryl Suasua.

2001: Hannah Myers, Annaleah Rush, Anna Richards, Lavinia Gould, Tamaku Paul, Toso Naoupu, Exia Shelford, Suzy Shortland, Vanessa Cootes, Dianne Kahura and Coach Darryl Suasua.

WALLAROO #19

After Hong Kong 2001, I returned to my new home in the Alice and new life amongst the members of the police team. The Northern Territory Institute of Sport had renewed my scholarship and I was able to continue flying backwards and forwards to either Darwin in the top end for games or Sydney to maintain my skills and match fitness. I am unsure how I managed to stay awake when I think back to those years of my life, especially whilst working shifts at the station. I either started work at 7am, 3pm or 11pm. The rostered shift was for eight hours but rarely did a police officer leave the station on time. There was no end to the work and sometimes shifts lasted longer than 24 hours.

My first 18 months was spent working as a probationary constable in general duties Alice Springs. These months exposed to me a number of different areas of police work, like the traffic unit, domestic violence unit, the juvenile task force, communications, working on the front counter and so on. I loved my job and the daily challenges and lessons of what was coming next (similar to rugby in many ways).

In 2001, we had a new national coach take over the Australian Wallaroos. Don Parry arrived on the scene and with him a new team (new manager Stephen Swan) and some old faces too. This was the team which would prepare players for the 2002 World Cup in Spain.

Our first national squad camp commenced on the 23rd of May, 2001, in Sydney. The team assembled at the Centra Camperdown. We had a few days to prepare for the first Test against the English ladies which was played at Eastwood on Saturday, 26th of May, 2001, at 3pm. This would be the first time ever that I switched playing positions. I appeared as #2 Elizabeth Andrew in the hookers role, a role that I was learning in the lead up to this game and the next World Cup.

Bob Hitchcock was assistant coach this year and it was Bob who chatted to me initially about moving positions in the forward pack. I had played my entire career at flanker (either open or blind side, meaning number 6 or 7) but I was happy to play anywhere (so long as it was in the forward pack). The game kicked off on time after the two national anthems and it was not long before the English ladies started to run over the top of us. We lost this game 41-19.

We had another week in between matches and this year, we also had an "Australia A" team alongside the Wallaroos. This effectively meant we had another full squad of Aussie girls trying to knock off the first XV for their position and for their World Cup jersey too. It was great for the sport and again, for the first time, we had competition to practice against our own sex and country (there would be no more having to play the U16 boys nor men from our Golden Oldies).

Our second match against the Poms was played in Newcastle on the Number 1 sports ground, NSW on Saturday, 2nd of June, 2001. We caught a bus from Sydney to Newcastle arriving about lunch time on game day. Kick off wasn't until 6pm so we had plenty of time to walk around, engage in a warm up, the girls who needed tape or strapping could get it and we would repeat same from the last weekend. Once again, we were beaten by the better team, losing 15-5. These two games and the time spent together in the camp was the longest the team, in my playing history, had spent together prior to an international game. It was great preparation for Spain the following year. We still had so much to learn and experience to gain. The English women were impressive (and scary) and some of the team were professionally paid, full time women's rugby players.

The 3rd-6th of November, 2001, were the dates for my next national rugby camp commitment. This was the next stage for selectors to choose the squad of 26 women to represent the Wallaroos in Spain in May 2002. The full squad of 44 players needed to be cut down significantly and these high numbers afforded the coaches and selectors with two women's teams to choose from.

The squad was divided into two even teams of 22 players. These teams played against each other in a trial match at the Greenway Oval, Canberra on Sunday, 5th of November, 2001. The squad, in the days before and after this match, trained hard at the AIS multipurpose fields where the pressure was on and at a pretty high level. For four days, the full squad resided at the Australian Institute of Sport competed for the 26 positions on the team. It was weird for me to be back in my hometown of Canberra yet residing at the AIS. I had celebrated my 30th birthday on the day before Wallaroo Camp. At 30, I was about average age within the playing ranks of our Wallaroo team. My body and mind were physically as ready as I could have ever possibly been for the last tournament of my playing history.

We had four months in between the camp at the AIS and the commencement of the World Cup. During this time and for months prior to this date, I completed a "World Cup training diary". It was a spreadsheet that I created myself to track my heart rate, body weight, hours of sleep, type of sleep, morning training, afternoon training, quantity of line out practice throws (a minimum of 100 per day), my menstrual cycle, my mood and one blank column titled "other". I religiously completed this diary which allowed me to keep track of me and keep me motivated.

2002

11th of March was the date when the 2002 Wallaroos team was announced – the team to be taken to the 4th International Women's Rugby World Cup in Barcelona, Spain. I thank God for a surname beginning with A, as I never had to wait long to either hear or not hear my name be called. I had made it! I was going to Spain for what would be my very last rugby tournament (until 2025 when we commence our Golden Oldies campaign in Singapore).

The squad assembled on the 4th of May, 2002, for a four-day camp at the Academy of Sport in Narrabeen, Sydney. There was plenty of work to be undertaken before flying out to see if we could perform better than we had done in 1998 when we achieved 5th place worldwide. Our results weren't bad for a nation who had only started playing the sport five minutes before the majority of the teams at Amsterdam. We Wallaroos wanted to improve our results and play the best rugby we could, and we all knew that the future of our game was riding on our performance.

A TRUCKLOAD OF 15S AND 7S RUGBY

On the 8th of May, 2002, the following people departed Sydney bound for Barcelona, Spain: Penny Anderson, Elizabeth Andrew, Ianthe Astley-Boden, Alyssa Campbell, Louise Cooke, Davina Craft, Gen Delves, Jennifer Egan, Louise Ferris, Lisa Fiola, Mieke Gladwin, Alex Hargraves, Debby Hodkinson, Bronwyn Laidlaw, Melissa Latu-Lutui, Bronnie Mackintosh, Sharon O'Kane, Tui Ormsby, Nyree Osieck, Pearl Palaialii, Naomi Roberts, Charmain Smith, Cheryl Soon, Bec Wakim, Nicole Wickert and Selena Worsley. Our management team included: Don Parry, Head Coach; Mr Bob Hitchcock, Assistant Coach; Stephen Swan, Manager; Scott Burn, Doctor; Hatie Brown, Physio; Craig Robberds, Trainer and Ben Whitaker; ARU Representative.

The Women's Rugby World Cup took place from the 13th-25th of May, 2002, in Barcelona, Spain. 16 teams were divided in to 4 pools in accordance with their seeding.
Pool A: New Zealand, Australia, Wales and Germany
Pool B: USA, France, Kazakhstan, Netherlands
Pool C: England, Spain, Japan, Italy
Pool D: Canada, Scotland, Samoa, Ireland.

The first 2 rounds of the tournament consisted of games between teams in the same pool. Winners of Round 1 then played in Round 2 for 1st or 2nd place in each pool and the losers played off for 3rd and 4th place in each pool.

Our first game in the tournament was 13th of May, 2002. We played against Wales in our opening game and won 30-0, it was the perfect start. Our second game was on the 17th of May against New Zealand, which, guess what? We lost 36-3 (but we gained some points at least given NZ destroyed Germany in their opening game 117-0)!

On the 20th of May we played our third game against the USA women (a very similar team whom had toured to Oz in the lead up) and won! The final score in that match was 17-5.

During our final match, for the plate (a competition for 5th and 6th place overall), we came up against Scotland at Girona. We won this final match

30-0 and I scored the very last try of the game. It was the perfect end to my international playing career for the Wallaroos (left hand corner). I was satisfied!

I felt ready to hang up my boots and wander back into my role as a police constable in the Yuendumu Community located about 300km west of Alice Springs. Another exciting chapter of my life awaited and I could hardly wait to get into the challenges of remote policing.

Massive thanks to the Australian Rugby Union for the support and the belief in us women, which eventually came and exactly when the time was right. Thanks to NSW Women's Rugby Union for allowing me to play in your weekend competition. Without that ability and acceptance of my registration, I would never have been able to qualify for the 2002 Women's Rugby World Cup Squad.

Thanks to NTIS and NTRU for all of the support over the years I was a member of your union. To South Darwin Rugby and NTRU and all within, I am truly grateful.

Thanks also to WARU and the women's committee, who again, allowed me to join your state when I was literally a "fly in, fly out" squad member. Thanks for the great memories and the tournament back to the east coast.

Finally, thanks goes to ACTRU, Wests Rugby and Royals Rugby who took me in, taught me a lot and allowed me to be a part of this wonderful journey. It is impossible to try and thank every man, women and child who supported me on my journey and who assisted in making it possible. Royals Rugby Union are celebrating 75 years of rugby in 2024. Royals were instrumental in kicking off the women's game in Canberra. It has been a privilege to wear the jersey and represent this club from my earliest playing days. I celebrated my 21st birthday within the old club at Weston and my 50th birthday at the temporary club house at Phillip Districts. The club will forever hold a very special place inside my heart, as do so many of the legends, both male and female within.

A TRUCKLOAD OF 15S AND 7S RUGBY

World Cup 2002 Barcelona, Spain

LEAGUE VERSUS UNION

I thought it was important to explain to the reader some of the differences between the game of women's rugby league and women's rugby union. Although there are many similarities between the two codes, the differences are equally as similar. The common denominator is rugby with an aim in both games of scoring the most amount of points to win. Rugby can be played socially and competitively and full side as well as reducing team numbers to seven in rugby union and nine in rugby league.

Both codes of rugby are classified as a sport where two teams try to score points by carrying an oval ball across a line or kicking it over and between a set of posts.

The referee is in charge of both games along with some support crew (not only touch judges who run along the sidelines but also now technical support which permits technology to accurately assist the referee to watch a replay and make a decision).

The referee, being male or female, blows a whistle to start and stop play. Rugby league and rugby union are both played on a rectangular field with goal posts at each end. In Australia, these fields are usually covered in grass, except in the Northern Territory (central Australia) and potentially other desert areas of this nation, where sometimes, the surface is red dirt or desert sand. In these remote areas players are still enjoying the game in bare feet as opposed to larger centres and cities where studded or plastic studs are worn on the bottom of supportive boots. These boots can be worn to provide a better grip on the playing surface (which can assist greatly if you have the funds to purchase a pair).

The aim of each game is to score points by putting the ball on or just over the opponent's try line. This action is called a try. A try in both codes is worth points (4 points in rugby league and 5 points in rugby union). The team with the most points at the end of the game is deemed the winner. Evidently there is generally a winner or a loser, though there can also be a tie (or sometimes called a draw) when scores are level at game's end and neither side has won or lost. In some competitions extra time is allowed to try to establish a winner.

Winning brings a mixture of feelings to individual players and teams as well as coaching and administrative staff. Joy, happiness, satisfaction and pride can be felt for the winners. Sadly the opposite feelings can result in the losing team however the main aim of rugby is to play your best game and enjoy the experience with your mates. There are many lessons to be learned from playing rugby, and these are not only limited to the field. Everyone is encouraged to give rugby a try, it is a game that has a position for every type of person whether they choose a playing position, administrative, officiators, etc.

Following a try, a designated player of the team who scored will also attempt to gain more points by kicking the ball through the opponent's goal posts. We call this a goal, and these are worth 2 points each in both rugby codes. The ball must go through the posts and not either side, as well as going above the cross bar. A player can score additional points by kicking penalty goals, or field goals at other times during the game.

LEAGUE VERSUS UNION

A game is played by two teams. In rugby league there are 13 players on the field during the game and in rugby union there are 15. The game is usually played over two 40-minute halves however some games in the women's arena and junior ages have been reduced in minutes. There is nothing and no reason which prevents women from playing the full 40 minutes per half, equal to the adult men (aside from politics and old-fashioned rules and laws which are gradually changing).

Players form two "groups" within each team. Forwards are typically the stronger, larger players (but not always) who conduct the heavy work. In union these players wear low numbers on the back of their playing jerseys and in league they wear higher numbers. The back line players called are "backs" opposed to forwards. Typically, (but not always) these players are lighter and faster than the forwards. These players are often magical members of the team who finish off the play, generally kick the ball and provide a different form of entertainment as opposed to the forwards (whom can equally amaze the crowds with their talents and skill in their specific roles). A combination of all players on the field and the two groups within each team make these sports amazing. Every player has their own responsibilities and roles. Reserve players can be substituted according to the laws of each game.

Rugby is an amazing game to play and equally as enjoyable for spectators. I strongly recommend that every person should give rugby a go as there is definitely a position and place for all people from every walk of life to find real mates and a tribe of people who will love you regardless of personalities, race, sexuality and all the rest of the issues that can divide us. All people are welcome and globally.

During the game, if your team has possession of the ball, you can only pass it backwards to your teammates and never forwards. You can pass the ball to one another as many times as you like until the person with the football is tackled. The player who is tackled then, in both codes, must hold on to the ball. There is a big difference in the two codes at this point.

In rugby league, when your team gets tackled six times in a row (while retaining possession for all six tackles), you then hand over possession of the ball to the opposition. The opposition then try to cross your line with their six opportunities to attack your line before possession is changed again. This renders rugby league a little more "structured" as opposed to rugby union where a team can dominate possession if they are more skilled in retention.

In rugby union, there is no limit to how many times a team is tackled, so long as your team retain possession of the ball and as long as they are moving in a forward direction. Their teammates are able to protect the ball and player however they must abide by the other laws (which are different in each game). In this respect and in my opinion only, this aspect of rugby union makes this game more technical and a different physical and mental challenge, in comparison to the game of rugby league. In both games, you are not permitted to tackle a player unless they have the ball.

A scrum is a part of both codes of rugby and during a scrum players from each team (six in rugby league and eight in rugby union) push against each other as the ball is placed on the ground in the middle of the front row of each scrum. The scrum is a contest for the ball. In rugby union the scrums are a battle for possession which can be stolen with good timing and accuracy, whereas rugby league mostly uses the scrum to restart play.

That voice inside my head is urging me to also advise you that scrummaging (and line outs) in rugby union is a highly technical and specialised skill that the forward pack acquire over time. Hours upon hours are spent practicing the fine art of the scrum and line out, both aspects of the game that allow the better team to win and also steal the ball during these periods of play. Further to this, a "scrum machine" is also a "thing" and another specialised piece of training equipment reserved for forwards only (forwards will know what I am talking about here). I won't go deeper into trying to explain to you the importance of learning how to safely scrummage in the game of rugby union, not only for safety reasons but to assist the team in winning the ball and therefore the game.

LEAGUE VERSUS UNION

There are many other aspects to each game (ruck, mauls, knock ons, etc), but I think this is enough information to help the reader differentiate between the two different codes of "footy" in Australia. There will always be an ongoing debate in Australia and possibly worldwide as to which game is better. My opinion is that both games are bloody great fun and can be the ultimate physical and mental test for any human being.

While not specifically related to the rules of the different rugby codes as such, these are some interesting facts about the games.

Legend has it that in 1823, during a game of school football in the town of Rugby, England, a young man named William Webb Ellis picked up the ball and ran towards the opposition's goal line. It was July 1829 that the first game of rugby was played in Australia between two men's teams.

The first female ever recorded playing rugby union was Irish born Emily Valentine, in the year 1887. The game was played in Northern Ireland and Emily was a young woman as opposed to an adult. It is possible that there were other girls also playing rugby union around this same era but Emily's story and involvement with the game remains the "earliest recorded written story". These were discovered in her written journals post her death.

It is believed that it was late in the 1930s that Australian women first started playing rugby union in country areas of NSW, Australia. Games came and went and for various and numerous reasons (not only due to war but possibly because the game was considered too rough and dangerous for women to play during these times). There are little records of who played when, the location and details of games, early photographs or how popular it may have been, etc. I believe, similar to my experience, that "girls just wanna have fun" the same as boys do and have had the privilege of for a greater length of time (until the 21st century anyway).

An established competition for women was not formally re-started until 1992 in Newcastle, NSW. An annual tournament for women has been played in Australia every year since then with the exception of during the covid-19 pandemic.

WALLAROO #19

The first international Test Match played between two women's international teams on Australian soil took place on the 2nd of September, 1994. This game was played between Australia and New Zealand in Sydney, with New Zealand claiming victory (which they have done upon every occasion ever since 1994 in a Test Match).

Aussie Gold were the first Australian sevens women's rugby team to enter the international sevens circuit at the Hong Kong tournament for women in 1997. Records for Australian women's sevens rugby, for some unknown reason, officially are only recorded since the inaugural Women's Sevens World Cup in 2009 (which was won by Australia). This issue is consistent with our nations worldwide and not just in Australia. It seems that unless tournaments were sanctioned by the IRB, they may not have been regarded as official results (the players and nations that did compete may argue that these results and records should be made official).

The Australian Wallaroos Women's Rugby Team played in their first International World Cup in 1998 in the Netherlands. The team came fifth. Australian Wallaroos have competed at every Women's Rugby International World Cup since our first. Our national sevens team has also competed in the Commonwealth Games and Olympics on every occasion that women were finally permitted the privilege of showcasing their skills in this sport too.

Rugby league's origins actually lie in the game of rugby union. In 1895 in England, rugby union teams from the north of England broke away from the country's Rugby Football Union and created their own union. This was called the Northern Rugby Football Union. This was a result of players being paid to play. The Northern Union created a newer version of rugby with different rules, creating a faster and more entertaining game to both play and spectate. This game is called rugby league and today is played by both sexes in Australia and is a fast-growing sport worldwide.

Men's rugby league was first played in Australia by men in 1907. Of the nine foundation teams that began in 1908, only two remain (South Sydney and the Sydney Roosters, who were originally called Eastern Suburbs).

LEAGUE VERSUS UNION

Similar to women's rugby union, women's rugby league in Australia also experienced fits of stops and starts over the past 100 years. The records for this sport are scarce and accurately documented histories are few and far between. What we do know is that the first women's rugby league match in Australia was played in Sydney, on Saturday, 17th of September, 1921. I have outlined this history in Chapter 3.

In the nation's capital, I know that rugby league for women again stopped and started in the 1980s. I first started playing rugby league in Canberra in 1991. The Canberra Women's Rugby League (CWRL) competition continued until the 2004 season.

The very first Australian "Foundation Team" was named in 1993 and was coached by John Squizzy Taylor (the same Squizzy who had coached me in NZ the previous year).

In 1995 the first AWRL National Championships were staged in Taree, NSW, with five teams competing. Illawarra met Canberra in the Grand Final and won the game 26-0. 1995 was the year in which the national team would be known as the Australian Women's Rugby League Team. It was not until another 12 months later that the national women's rugby league team would be called the Jillaroos (a similar experience to the naming of the Wallaroos).

It was in 1993 that the Australian Women's Rugby League was formed, with the Australian women's team being the Jillaroos. The definition of a jillaroo is a female who works on either a sheep or cattle station in Australia. Jillaroos playing for the Australian national team are highly talented and fit sportswomen (who may or may not work on cattle stations in their free time)! The name Jillaroo was chosen as it is the equivalent to the male term Jackaroo. It was important to the women who played the game that they were treated and seen as equals as well as being afforded the equal opportunities (which is a work in progress, but steady gains are being made).

In 1996, newcomers to the game of women's rugby league, Queensland, joined the fray. Sydney were winners that year, beating the Illawarra 8-4 in the Grand Final.

An annual tournament would be played for women's rugby league players to assist in developing this sport for women in Oz. The competition and playing base grew from strength to strength and rugby league, like union, is a fast-growing sport for girls and women in this era. The Katrina Fanning Shield (open women's rugby league) competition in Canberra commenced in 2017 and continues to this day.

Men's interstate football dates back to 1908 in Australia. It became known as State of Origin in 1980 and is often regarded the toughest, most demanding, most emotionally-charged contest in the game of rugby league. It has been, in more recent decades, an annual three-game battle played out between NSW and Queensland.

Every year since 1999 the women representative sides have also joined in this famous "State of Origin" (Women's Interstate Challenge) series within Australia. It was rebranded State of Origin in 2018. For the first time in Origin history, and at the time of sending my book to print, the women's State of Origin will take place over three games in 2024. The Maroons from Queensland are defending the shield following their points aggregate victory over the Blues in last year's controversial two-game series. The women playing this code of rugby league are performing on par with the men, the grandstand is packed, and fans are thoroughly enjoying watching the women play rugby league and it is magnificent to witness the growth and acceptance of females.

At the international level, teams play for the Women's Rugby League World Cup as well as on worldwide tours. The opportunities for women are increasing not only on the field but in the administrative areas, coaching, TV, officiating and more. It is becoming more common to see females commentating even men's games on TV and being recognised for their talents in all aspects of the game and promotion of it.

In the 1990s, television had a big impact on the men's version of rugby league when Rupert Murdoch and his News Corporation entered the picture and came up against James Packer. Both Murdoch and Packer sought exclusive television broadcasting rights for rugby league. The women's game avoided this ugly and costly battle resulting in the Super League which has benefitted the women's game immensely.

What I did learn from my own involvement in women's rugby and rugby league is that both are great games. Women have finally been afforded the opportunity to play many male-dominated sports worldwide. Various sports have a long and continuous history (e.g women's cricket and soccer), but other sports have not been so lucky. Change is happening and it is inspiring and welcome.

What is important to me, has been to provide the reader with some of the history of both games in Australia. I could only do this because I played a part in both codes, playing for the Australian Capital Territory as a representative player in both.

It is an extraordinary thought and fact that the history of women, playing either code of "footy" in this amazing country, already extends back more than one century. I hope and pray that the games will not experience the stops and starts that it endured over the past 100 years.

In 2021, Ali Donnelly wrote a book titled "Scrum Queens; The Story of Women's Rugby", Pitch Publishing 2022. Ali has done a superb job in documenting the story of women's rugby worldwide, including parts of her own English rugby story too. For any reader wanting to learn more about the game of rugby union for women, her book is a must. Congrats to Ali on documenting what you have been able to do thus far, particularly given the scarce history of our amazing game. Her website scrumqueens.com is a must visit for anyone interested in more about women's rugby.

In September 2022, Ruby Tui (a New Zealand Black Fern and women's rugby modern day legend) also published a book. The title is "Straight Up" and Ruby, like hundreds in NZ before her playing era, is a Kiwi superstar. She bravely shares an honest account of her life and her path to becoming an Olympic rugby union champion. One day, who knows, there may be many more books like Ruby's on the shelves in libraries documenting the lives of women's rugby players and some accurate history books too.

WALLAROO #19

I am hoping my own book has inspired at least one more player or even a historian out there to help preserve the history of our women's game. It has been far too important to me personally for it to be lost after all this effort.

LEARNINGS

In this chapter, I want to outline some of the learnings that rugby has provided me with. I've separated those into a few different sections in this chapter.

On the field

I learned the value of being part of a team, sometimes a small team of ten and other times a larger team of 22 or more. I learned how to play in a few different rugby positions from flanker (both sides of the scrum) right up to the front row in the hooker's role. At one women's national tournament I even played prop forward. I love the forwards, but I was not born to play in the back line! I learned that every position in every team was equally as important as the next one.

One of the biggest rugby lessons I would learn came on the day of our first international match, on the 2nd of September, 1994, when I was awarded with the #19, a reserve jersey and position on the bench. This was the first time in my entire life I had not made the "run on team" in any game and in any sport. I was shattered and it hurt, that old feeling of "not being good enough" returned and I didn't like it. I thought at the time that this was the worst experience of my sporting history. I felt ashamed of myself for not being good enough to make the top 15 and run onto the field to get the ball first. Shame was a feeling that I was familiar with from my childhood and teen years, so I knew this feeling well.

I didn't like the experience of sitting on that bench. I didn't want to look at the coach as I may have been tempted to place my bare hands around his neck (which I know was not a part of this game and could land me in prison). In fact, that night, I didn't even want my teammates to look at me nor speak to me during the warmup to try and make me feel "good enough". I bloody well didn't, and I just wanted to run away from all the training and effort I had put into that day and spit my dummy and return home. At the time, I just wanted to be invisible and stuff that green and gold #19 jersey down the toilet. That wasn't an option.

In hindsight, the part of me that played during that game and as a reserve, waiting for my call up into the game, remains an important part of me that needed to be discovered, nurtured and investigated further. Every team needs reserves, especially when our first 15 players need a break or become injured. I do believe it is important for the best team to be played, I also believe that when possible, all players on the bench should be afforded some time on the paddock. Again that comes down to the coach and I have had to respect the decisions and advice of every coach which I played under. The experience and the #19 was a good one for me. I would learn this after the fact not so much during the experience. I did get over it and clearly have learned to also love that part of me (which is probably one of the most important parts of my makeup). All parts are welcome, so they say! Today I love #19 and feel proud of that jersey and the fact that I was selected for the first ever test team.

I hope that in this modern era of rugby, we talk about the role of a reserve and how important they are in the team and at every level. Maybe that way,

LEARNINGS

we can reduce some of the shame possibly experienced by other players too. My own experience has been that when we share the shame and talk it through, it helps to break it down into a more manageable experience. I am guessing that everyone who trains on for a World Cup squad wants to play and in the first XV but I only know my own experience. I like single digits on my jerseys but the fact that my first ever Australian Test Match jersey had the #19 meant that I needed to embrace the number (and face it by also placing it in the title of this book). Besides, it is now my Wallaroo identity and I am not only grateful for the number but feel proud to be #19.

Fortunately for me, that evening of our first international Test against the Kiwis, I did get onto the paddock and early in the game. Missing those first 15 minutes of that match, not getting the jersey I dreamt of these were lessons that were very good for my development into adult life, not just a part of this historic rugby game.

The jerseys that I kept in my collection range from numbers 1-19. I kept the ones that were special to me and had some of these framed with the team photos too (especially the World Cups). My sevens jerseys collection included all types of numbers; in 1997 I wore #3, 1999 I wore #9 and so on.

On each occasion whilst typing this book, I have worn a different jersey every time I sat here to type, to remember, to laugh, to look through the scrap books and enjoy being back in a jersey that holds so many precious memories for me. These are not only the Aussie jerseys from so many games, teams and the two World Cups, these also include the Arabian Gulf, Scotland, the New Zealand Wild Ducks, USA, Spain and numerous others that I kept and still wear (many have fallen apart and gone to the rag bag or only reserved for gardening).

To be honest, I never wore that All Blacks jersey whilst typing this book on my laptop. Maybe it would have been bad luck or sacrilegious to my values, it just doesn't sit well in any respect. That NZ jersey remains in pristine condition on the hanger in the back of my cupboard like a big black hairy spider. I have probably worn that jersey less than three times since I swapped it with the hooker at the 2002 World Cup in Spain (I also have the NZ #19 which I must have swapped in 1994 too). I guess I keep it for memories' sake, not so much to wear it (given it only brings back loss and grief). That Black Ferns jersey is the only one in my entire collection without a rip nor grass stain on it (those Kiwis were pretty hard to catch in my day)!

Another of the many lessons learned on the field over those ten years of my playing life was that all I had to do was play my position and concentrate on that. If I was worried that someone in my team wasn't fulfilling their role, that wasn't my issue because if I didn't play my role, there would be a gap and that pesky first five eighth would wander straight through our line and score. My job wasn't to play two positions, it was to focus on my opposition, listen to the captain and referee, play my best and most of all enjoy all 60 or 80 minutes. If someone made a mistake or couldn't match up to their opponent or do their own specific job on the field, I could cover and try to help out (which happens through the entire game of union) but that wasn't my primary focus. I was pretty committed back then, today I am pretty sure I would be falling off tackles and watching the opposition run right past me.

I never really enjoyed nor chased the responsibility of being a captain in a team I played for. I don't think I had enough brain power, knowledge of the game nor vision to undertake this role very well. I just preferred to get out onto the field and leave the calls, organising and all the rest up to someone else – besides, most of my playing career was alongside Loui Ferris and trust me, no one speaks when that woman starts barking orders. She had an amazing grasp on every game we played together and no doubt, is the best player of my career (as well as a great friend). The same goes for Helen Taylor, another great captain in my playing career while in the ACT and in the early years of my rugby development for Australia. Louise and Helen were an amazing combination of talent in the half and first five eight positions. Thank you, girls, for all you taught me and all of the amazing memories. Thanks also to every other girl whom I played these amazing games with, it honestly was amazing and provided me with some of the best fun and years of my life.

LEARNINGS

On the field, there were a lot of rules called laws of the game. Once I learned these, I could respond during the game quickly and keep the ball alive and moving. Undertaking the referee's course early on in my career and later on (1997) doing my Coaching Level I and II was really valuable learning for me. It is with thanks to Wests Rugby Union in Canberra (Ken Sutherland specifically) who funded both Sharrin and I to obtain our coaching qualifications. Sharrin and I started up the West Women's Rugby Union side in Canberra for the 1997 women local season. Sharrin was the coach, and I was captain, and I am unsure how we managed to field a whole new team that season, but we did, and it expanded the competition from the originals being Royals, then ANU and eventually Tuggeranong Vikings, Wests and so on.

I played a lot of rugby. I loved all the training, the games and travel too. Every training session, team meeting, game, all of it taught me things about myself. What I played and trained through helped to shape the adult I was growing into being. Rugby helped me to build and retain some amazing relationships with teammates, coaches, admin staff and others. Rugby was a big part of me learning about what I could achieve personally and collectively.

On the field I learned that I could physically push my body and mind. I never blacked out due to heat, exhaustion, dehydration, overuse or any of the other issues that I witnessed other girls deal with whilst playing. I was never one of those players who vomited on the sideline during the half time break, I had the ability to keep on playing and trying (I am guessing this comes of the generations of amazing strong women in my heritage, specifically my grandmothers Mary (Molly) and Shelia – both legends). I had my routines and schedules and stuck to what I knew worked best for me. This got easier with experience and my mental toughness got stronger as I believed more and more in my own ability to just keep on pushing myself when others just gave up. I guess it is my nature and maybe my childhood, teen years and genetics were just the right combination. I have always felt blessed too.

Physically, mentally, and spiritually I learned many lessons in these young adult years of my life. These would help me to deal with the years that were yet to come and all the challenges that life afforded me.

WALLAROO #19

I was raised in a family where religion was part of our daily lives. To my parents, this was of high importance as it was to their own parents and the era of Australian history when the influence of the Irish Catholics was great. Back then, religious persons were identified by wearing these unusual clothes and head dresses. It was just accepted that this was the way it was and this dress was required to set them apart. I thank my parents for the faith which influenced my own adult beliefs and now the freedom to make my own choices.

On the day of my birth, I arrived in a gay and joyful kind of way. From my earliest memories, I was never interested in boys, not in the way my mates were anyway. By the time I reached my teen years and puberty finally arrived at about 15 years, I had a nasty reality check with my head and the religious beliefs of my family (and every adult who surrounded and supported me). I was gay and I had nowhere to turn nor anyone in the world to speak to about the topic. Shame and self-abandonment arrived and still visit to this day but I learned to ride the waves of feelings – feelings that would come and go until footy arrived in my world along with my first female partner in 1994. Prior to commencing sport in this new game (initially rugby league), I had never spoken to anyone about my sexuality. Both codes of rugby helped me to accept that I was born exactly the way my God had intended. I had finally found a home in women's rugby, where I felt accepted and where I fit in. What a bloody relief.

Those middle years of my league career brought with it the freedom to explore my sexuality and an intimate relationship with a woman. I did try and do the heterosexual thing before and after this relationship. Thank you to Richard and Tony for the good times and for your patience with me. I knew deep down that wasn't being the true me if I stayed with a guy for the sake of my family and pleasing other adults. Without stumbling across the game of women's rugby, where I met my first gay friends, I am unsure how my sexuality might have evolved. I had many heterosexual friends who were married because it was the "normal" thing to do, even though all that did was create upset for many. I am grateful for the blessings and the friends from my early footy days who helped me work myself out (as that wasn't easy and remains an ongoing process). Rugby felt like a place

LEARNINGS

where the level of judgement was less, and all players were accepted as part of the team in the state they arrived on game day. I thank God for footy, my mates but mostly for acceptance in the footy family and worldwide.

Rugby league and union, like most other women's sports that I have played in Oz, had a percentage of gay players. I would not say this was any more in the rugby codes than I came across in other sports, nor would I agree that gay women are attracted to contact sport. I think women who like rugby, play rugby and their sexuality has nothing to do with that.

The other point that is useful to make here is that, just because I am gay, doesn't mean that I am attracted to every female in this amazing world. I have been attracted to just three special women in my life thus far, all very different women and all who will hold a unique place in my heart and story. To Ronnie, Sharrin and Mylie, thank you for the lessons and the loving.

In the training arena

I learned that there is no substitute for hard work and commitment. These pay off. From the outset and particularly once I was selected in the 1993 Development Team, I wanted to be the best I could. I decided to leave a paid job with ACT Health, to train full time and forgo a salary. That is how much this sport and the opportunity meant to me at the time. I was 22 years old and was in a period of my life where I could prioritise what I wanted to do with my life and my love of sport. I saw the opportunity and took it.

My great mate Loui Ferris did the same. She also quit her work in the public service, and we trained each other, meeting at the Royals' training ovals in Rivett every second day and supplementing this with weight training, cardio work, swimming, and ball skills. I had some catching up to do (as I didn't come from a touch footy nor oztag background like a lot of my teammates) and I had no idea (and still don't) about that thing called stepping! Loui taught me a lot during those months in the lead up to our very first international Test Match. Gosh we were committed and surrounded by some amazing teammates. The other important thing to note here is the quality of coaches I had access to. I believe that a great team will blossom under the right guidance. Fortunately for me, I had great coaching right from the beginning, not only in my mate and first rugby league coach Loui but the likes of Graham Willard, Squizzy Taylor, Col Spence and Bob Hitchcock among so many others.

I owe a huge thank you to my teammates from every team, club and organisation, especially those originals from the East Canberra and Royals rugby union and Australian Wallaroos and Aussie Gold teams. Those girls that surrounded me on the training oval and playing paddock helped me develop into the player I became, and without their skills and enthusiasm, I would not have got to the level which I did. I am looking forward to my next journey with the Golden Oldies in Singapore 2025. God only knows what the Wobblyroos can do on the other side of 50 years but I am looking forward to participating.

Moving to the Northern Territory at the end of the 1997 was highly beneficial to my playing career (and life). It opened so many doors and opportunities for me, brought so much travel, training, games, friendships and employment roles. I give thanks to Shelley Lingman, Shirley Russel and the crew of Darwin women and men that made those years so special and so much fun.

Off the field

The lessons kept on coming. The more games and tournaments I participated in during my playing years, the more and more I learned and the more people I met. In every single town and country, in every team, I came across people with similar characteristics. This stood out. Rugby people were committed to their teams and clubs. Being part of this meant you became part of a worldwide family, not just a team in the back suburbs of Weston Creek. It meant you belonged. I also know that worldwide, I can show up at a rugby field and find the same. Someone who

LEARNINGS

would help me out if I needed anything. This was consistent everywhere I went all around the world.

The game and my experiences from 1991 until 2002, when I retired after the Spanish World Cup, set me up to handle life's challenges. I knew that physically I could push my body to a limit that felt without a finish line. I could always and would always keep trying, even when I thought I couldn't do one more hill sprint, one more burpie, one more run up the field with the ball, one more tackle, somehow I found the energy deep inside of me to keep on pushing myself. That energy comes from a part inside of me that I have discovered is a true part of me. Rugby helped me to learn about myself.

That "part" of me wanted to be seen, acknowledged, and congratulated, even if I wasn't aware of this at the time. This was something that I desired from my childhood but which went amiss amongst the large and busy family in which I was raised. Rugby gave that "part" inside of me love and the longer I played the more aware I became of who I wanted to be in the world. I am grateful to my rugby family for providing me with this platform and for helping me to learn all that I have so far. Writing this book has helped me to see things that were not obvious at the time too, and for that I am also grateful.

All those years of training and playing taught me to "never give up", regardless of what I was doing. This experience helped me greatly throughout the ten years of my police career, then into my adult years as a mother. The challenges of life keep on coming but the past has helped me to know that I am capable of achieving great things if I really try hard and refuse to give in.

One thing to also note in reference to the female body, from my experience in a female body. I do not believe that there are any greater risks to the body of a women opposed to that of male players. Given the age of women's rugby in Australia and the lack of history within the ranks, including the consistent underfunding, medical research and reporting has not been officially gathered to prove or disprove that a female body is not designed for the game. Over the ten-year period of playing rugby, I injured my right knee and tore my ACL, I broke my left-hand ring finger and my nose over and over. I had little physio and no surgery for any injury related to rugby. After retiring from the sport and engaging in operational policing for 10 years (where I wasn't chasing Gilbert but thousands of others), I didn't experience injury and maintained fitness and weight training. I went on to give birth to four healthy babies and enjoyed uncomplicated pregnancies. Although I suffered with mastitis during breastfeeding my four sons, I have not had any issues with my reproductive organs nor breasts.

With thanks

To the organisers of the local Canberra Women's Rugby League Competition in 1991, the president of that era Gerry Edwards who allowed women to participate, to the sponsors, the volunteers, the referees, "the men who made the decision to open the gate". Special mention to a great man and referee Lionel Hart who taught me a lot and showed up for match after match with his pain in the butt whistle and humour!

To the coaches from those early years who helped to teach me how to play. Mr Graham Willard, his dedicated wife Penny and John Squizzy Taylor. These men were volunteers that believed in us. Just like the playing group, they had some amazing fun, saw some great rugby and made some amazing friendships and memories.

Big shout goes out to all the ladies who formed the first ever ACT Women's Rugby League Committee and all sponsors and supporters. Thanks for getting the ball rolling. It is amazing to see the growth in the game of women's rugby league and to be able to sit back, watch and enjoy the games, free to air! Congrats ladies.

Helen Wylks was the women responsible for "finding me" and introducing me to the game of league. Helen and I journeyed together into the game of rugby union via Royals Rugby and today, she remains a legend, one of the most genuine and amazing people and gifted athlete, photographer

LEARNINGS

(among other talents) I have met. Thank you, Helen, for your persistence to finally get me to West Belconnen that morning, and invite me to join East Canberra. This game changed the course of my adult life.

Peter and Lannie Pomazak were our trusted financial sponsors, friends, managers, substitute coaches and generally an amazing couple. Pete was like a father to us all and Lannie a mother. Without Pete and Lannie's financial contribution in those early years of both women's rugby league and union in Canberra, we may never have been able to field a team nor last the distance. Our game may have died out with your financial backing Pete. The generosity of Pete and Lannie will never be forgotten, nor will those amazing and fun times, especially the parties. These two are and always will be absolute legends of the women's game. Wherever you two got to, I will never forget you. Thanks.

Thanks to the girls. My first team ever playing for East Canberra (which later became the Canberra Breakaways) in the ACT Women's Rugby League Competition of 1991 was made up of: Anna Willcock, Helen Wylks, Carole Simpkins, Katrina Maddon, Darlene Riley, Kylie Baker, Glenda Merritt, Louise Ferris, Megan Mitchell and Carolyn Walshe. A team of legends (in my eyes anyway and some good old fun).

In those early years, it would be true to say that every single one of us contributed to developing and growing the game. We sold raffle tickets (usually alcohol as the prize), endless boxes of chocolates, frozen chickens, and meat trays to raise the funds to travel and play. We did these things as a unit, helping each other, supporting, and growing on and off the field. I feel proud to have played a few roles within those early years of my league playing days as President of the ACT Women's Rugby League, Tour Organiser of the NZ trip in 1992, fundraiser and team member. I undertook a course in Sports Administration and learned a lot more than I ever anticipated. I feel blessed and grateful to have served the CWRL, played and most of all enjoyed every moment of the experience. The Statesmen Motel in Curtin were a sponsor for years and we all enjoyed many a drink, the odd arm-wrestling competition and loads of fun in that establishment.

It is impossible for me to list everyone who helped me throughout my playing career – there were so many players, coaches, trainers and mates. I am hoping that "thank you" might cover you all.

When I switched across from rugby league to union, I found a whole new team, new staff, new clubs, and new experiences. The feeling was same but different. My union career started in the Royals Rugby Union. I thank the team, and the men Paul Cornish, Matthew Brennan and Wayne McCauliffe for their investment in our ACT Wallaroos team in that very first tournament for women held in Newcastle, NSW in 1992. Without the support of Royals Rugby, the loan of the bus, the men involved at training, coaching, the licenced premises, the wonderful Anne and Peter (Rabbits) Gallagher for the sports training and strapping, bus driving and various support, we possibly would not have made those events as good as they were. Kym Thurbon, Dougal Whitton, Brian Bourke, Andy Clark, there are too many amazing men to single out who helped and supported women's rugby along the journey from 1992 and still to this day.

Col Spence (coach of Royals Women and ACT) volunteered years of his life and made a big commitment to our women's team and game. Thank you, Col. Dougal Whitton is a legend of the club and of course the Pomazak pair followed us from league into union too. Bob Shakespeare has and remains to be a legend, always present and always giving service. I thank them all for their commitment and passion to the women's game and blue bloods.

The coaches in my first ever national camp included Mick Willis, Paul Cornish and Rob Bradley (employed by the ARU at the time as the National Development Co-ordinator). Bob Hitchcock and Joan Forno were present in my rugby playing career from the first year of my involvement with rugby and were both standing with me on the day of my final game in Spain at the Women's Rugby Union World Cup in 2002. They are legends, both along with Shelley Lingman who worked tirelessly with her band of volunteers to get women's rugby in the NT moving and growing.

Don Parry (Coach) and Stephen Swan (Manager) were the major players in the 2002 World Cup when the Wallaroos toured to Spain and came

LEARNINGS

home with that bloody plate again. I am unaware how much work goes into preparing a team of women who are spread across a nation as large as ours, but I am guessing it's a mountain. Neither of these men I knew very well, Don was a Queenslander and Swannie a NSW man, but both were clearly dedicated to our mission of heading to Spain with the intention of winning the Women's Rugby World Cup. I wish to thank them both for their service to that tour and all they did for me personally. To Swannie, I remain sorry if my actions and involvement with the fire extinguisher on the second last morning of our tour got you or the team into any heat, I honestly could not resist that opportunity nor the fun. I still maintain that I was doing it for the team and just trying to sober up a teammate that was about to miss her international flight! I know it was a very naughty thing to do but gosh it felt good (and sobered her up)! Thanks gents and the whole team who took us to Spain: Bobby Hitchcock, Dr Scott Burn, Craig Robberbs and Ben Whitaker. Shout also goes out to our team physio Hatie Brown.

There is another amazing lady who deserves recognition from my era. Her name is Goldie. Christine Gold was one of the early managers of the Australian Wallaroos and also took on many other club and representative roles in Queensland Rugby. Goldie is one of those rugby legends whose christian name few people rarely knew, yet she was golden and remains so. Goldie, your service to women's rugby was outstanding (as were your hugs when any of us needed one). You were and are still very much loved by us all. Thank you for everything you did for women's rugby nationwide. You are amazing and we are all grateful.

To all the coaches: there are too many to list, but they know who they are, from the Australian Wallaroos and Aussie Gold to the ACT, NT, WA and NSW state teams. To all the support crew, the assistant coaches, the managers, the sports trainers, physios and admin crew who made and contributed to my playing career. Thank you.

Thanks goes to the ACT Academy of Sport in Canberra for the first scholarship in 1996 and the Australian Institute of Sport, Australian Sports Commission and all sponsors and funding bodies who made this all possible.

WALLAROO #19

Thanks to the Northern Territory Institute of Sport; both Darwin and Alice Springs offices, staff and personnel. The director of the NTIS during my time in sport was Dr Dennis Hatcher; he was amazing, and acknowledged every single one of my team selections in writing with a letter of congratulations. I felt very supported by the NTIS team which included but was not limited to Andrew Modra, Kym Thurbon, Leon Zagorskis, Pat Bree, and Graham Reed. I remain grateful.

My parents deserve a thanks. Without them, I wouldn't have ever had one gasp of oxygen nor a life, and I certainly would not be writing this book. Mum and Dad both travelled around this country to watch and support me playing when they could. Mum, without a doubt, is the biggest sporting fanatic of all and my biggest fan throughout my entire career and life. I love my mum in a special way. She also fed and clothed me along with Dad, who provided for my every need during my childhood, my education and beyond. Parenting seven children is not an easy task and they have performed the best they could. Right at the end of my playing career, some of the women's games were televised. Finally, Mum got to sit in her comfy chair in the lounge room in the old home in Duffy, watching me on TV and listening to the commentary via ABC radio on that trusty trannie. Thanks Mum and Dad for everything (and not just footy). I love you both dearly and feel grateful for everything you have done for these four precious boys and I.

Huge thanks goes to my ex-partner Sharrin. We met at a rugby event in Sydney in 1996 and enjoyed some of the best years of our lives together. My entire playing career occurred during our 23 year relationship. From ACT to NT, to Holland, Africia, Spain and Honkers four times over. I could not have continued to play and train without your love, interest, support and passion for the game of rugby.

A final word of thanks goes to my dearly loved ones: Mylie, for your on going love and support. My four sons John, Matthew, Stuie and Daniel, none of whom ever got to see me play footy. All of whom I love dearly and who fill my days with joy.

11

LEAVING MY FOOTPRINT

My rugby experiences, along with my life thus far assisted my growth as a human being, not just a rugby player. These experiences shaped and contributed to my adult life. I believe am lucky, I also know I created and worked hard for the opportunities that were afforded to me. Throughout the ten years of my rugby days, I did feel loss, I did miss out on final playoffs, I did miss out on the first XI and I did have the experience of warming the bench. All of these experiences were good for my growth, even those times when I didn't like the feelings associated with the experiences.

Writing this book has helped me to see the influence that my rugby experience, all of it, had on the future chapters of my life. I feel grateful that rugby brought parts of me to the surface, parts which have stuck with me and helped me to grow into the adult that achieved many things. I feel grateful for the education I was given and all the people who influenced my life, especially those closest to me.

I had a full childhood, growing up in Australia, the wide brown land, which allowed me to run free and enjoy being an Aussie kid eating vegemite on toast and drinking clean drinking water from the tap and sometimes the hose. This was the first decade of my life, including an introduction to a sport called netball and school mates, whom I am still in contact with 45 years later.

The second decade brought with it my teen years and the opportunity to find new sports and a larger circle of friends. I grew away from my family and tested the waters in the big wide world. I continued to try other sports and started to travel the world with my pushy and backpack. Being a teenager can really suck, it is a big transition from childhood into puberty and an entry into adult life. I am pleased to learn and experience more open communication between kids and parents in the 21st century where kids are free to discuss hard subjects with greater freedom and honesty than the good old days (which were great in some respects but damaging in plenty of other ways). My kids have the ability to freely talk, trust and feel which can only be a good thing.

I was in my early 20s when I first played rugby in 1992. The next decade of my life was filled with the previous chapters of this book (and a whole lot more). I hope I have shared a little glimpse of the fun I had, the mates I discovered and the countries I visited.

For the decade which followed my rugby career, I enjoyed another decade within the ranks of NT police. I lived and worked in five different remote locations during this period. I discovered that policing was just as much fun as rugby had been, yet a unique and possibly greater mental challenge. Trust me, I still needed to be fit to give chase and tackle from behind at times, as well as to jump the odd high fence and stay awake long enough to drive a prisoner on a long journey to a major centre!

The police job tested me. Whilst serving at Australia's most remote police station in the Gibson desert (Kintore or Warlungurru) I would receive my first promotion and second stripe to Senior Constable. Sadly, there are no winners in the game of operational policing. The role is demanding in body, mind and spirit and decisions and actions, just like a rugby game, need to be made in a split second at times. These decisions can win or lose a game and can have a serious impact on not just their situation, but a victim or offenders' life.

My role as a general duties cop ranged from juvenile taskforces, the domestic violence unit, the traffic and highway unit and so much more. In every role and every unit, most days were filled with trauma, tragedy, suicide, violence and some of the most horrendous experiences that you might imagine. I am unsure if police recruits can really ever be prepared for what might happen on that first shift of their operational careers. There is one difference between rugby and my police role; even if you physically were injured on the field, the effects of the traumas I witnessed as a police officer would be long-lasting and require some hard work further down the track unpacking the gift of PTSD.

Those childhood and teen years, plus the ten years playing rugby, set me up as a capable cop. I was able to back myself and my physical abilities (even though I am not blessed with height), and be confident in the decisions that I made in the spur of the moment. I did conduct myself in the best way I could, given the situations I found myself in, every day of my career. I loved being a cop, it was a privilege and again, something I took seriously (especially having to prosecute my own court files in the bush court).

The chapters which included my childhood, teen years, rugby experience and police career would all prepare me adequately for this current chapter of my life – the best one thus far. Motherhood.

My eldest son, John, was born in Alice Springs Hospital in January 2007. The pregnancy was uncomplicated and of course, I grabbed another record becoming NT's first female cop to work operationally in a remote station until two weeks before giving birth. My pregnancy was unnoticed until about five months when I declared my news to the superintendent. I loved being pregnant and didn't need one day of sick leave throughout that period either (I can hear my good friend Jenny saying that I booked off for a meal break and gave birth and returned to work before the end of that shift!). It was actually a period of three months maternity leave before I returned to my role as Brevet Sergeant of the Ali Curung Police Station.

20 weeks before son #2 arrived in November 2008, our little family of three, plus little dog called Ally, re-located to civilisation and returned to my hometown Canberra to be closer to family. Matthew arrived in a hurry and was almost caught by our midwife in the carpark of Canberra hospital. This labour lasted less than one hour and there was no fuss nor mess, we were all home by lunchtime to enjoy our little almond-eyed boy and marvel at the true knot that had been located in the umbilical cord during his birth.

Stuart was birth #3, arriving in the early hours of the morning right before the canonisation of Australia's first and only saint, Mary MacKillop, on the 17th of October, 2010. This baby and his first 13 years of his life have been filled with the joy that equals his huge smile and warmth that he brings to every single day. In April 2024, Stuie commenced his first season of rugby league. The U14 Rams boys have already seen Stuie score his first try (and he didn't drop the ball over the try line but fully stretched out and scored his first ever try, dragging two opponents hanging off his lower body) and leg lift a poor young kid in a tackle that was beautiful to watch. That's my boy (well one of the four)!

Son #4, Daniel, brought with him, on the day of the 20-week ultrasound, a report that he was bearing a rare congenital heart defect. A new and unfamiliar challenge emerged instantly. Bang – life changed instantaneously, and a new type of fear arrived.

Daniel arrived by the same method as his three older brothers but this time at the Westmead Children's Hospital, Sydney. Ronald McDonald House and this hospital would become a home away from home for the next four years while we stepped into a new and unfamiliar world of cardiology, hospitals and the most amazing nursing care ever.

During the first five years of Daniel's life, everything about my life changed. I guess that has been the one guarantee that life has taught me thus far.

Nothing stays the same, everything changes (and thank God for change, not so much the heart defect!).

Daniel underwent three major heart surgeries, as well as three other operations to attempt to assist his system cope and of course, keep him alive. Although these were all part of the early challenges of his life, it wasn't too shabby for a baby that was not supposed to be "compatible with life". We never, never know!

Daniel made it this far and we all survived with huge thanks to my mum, who held the fort in my own family home, time after time during all of my absences. The support and prayers of so many people, including my ex-partner, my biological family and friends will always be appreciated, as well as the beautiful staff at St Anthony's Primary School, Wanniassa.

During this chapter of my mid-40s, after Daniel's Fontan circulation was completed, I further, just to add a little more challenge into my life, embarked on a career as a single parent.

Not only could I not find a Gilbert (nor keep my eyes open or awake after I had put the last boy to bed), but I also no longer had a glock nor taser (which trust me I could have used just for target practice and to release some resentment)! What I did have were all of the previous life experiences, confidence in myself, the lessons, the learnings, the training, the nutrition, family support, long-term friends, rugby networks and of course, belief in and a relationship with a power greater than me (I thank God for my God).

This wraps up what I consider the first half of my life. It's been a pleasure to share this journey with you. There remains some parenting on the horizon and some fun mothering yet to be done until these four young men have all been educated and encouraged out into the adult world. On this significant 30-year Wallaroo anniversary, I have three teenage sons in the house as well as one tween. I pray for God's help to get me through this next decade and use all the learnings of my life to date.

WALLAROO #19

Happy anniversary to each and every Wallaroo on the 2nd of September, 2024. Well done to all who made this happen, especially the Australian Rugby Union. Good luck to all future players in Australia and worldwide. I hope you enjoy the sport as much as I did.

Love Lib
Wallaroo #19

CAREER TIMELINES

My rugby timeline

1991: Played in my first game of "footy", women's rugby league for East Canberra. Played my first representative game for ACT Women's Rugby League. Played in exhibition match Bruce Stadium, ACT. Long distance bike riding this year included: Sydney to Melbourne, Sydney to Wollongong, plus local riding and lots of it.

1992: Played in East Canberra Women's Rugby League Team (first year I played the entire season). Attended the inaugural Women's Rugby Union Challenge, in Newcastle, NSW. Played representative rugby league for the ACT and travelled to New Zealand for my first international rugby league tour (North Island). Engaged in ACT women's arm-wrestling tournament, won ACT title (open women's). Overseas adventure to USA, UK and Eastern Europe. Played women's rugby union in various locations and countries during this trip.

WALLAROO #19

1993: Continued playing women's rugby league in Canberra local competition and various representative games in various locations. Returned to Newcastle for second Annual Women's Rugby Union Championships. Selected in first Australian Women's Rugby Union Development Squad and participated in inaugural Development Camp for women's rugby union in Newcastle. Invited back to arm wrestling championship, Canberra and won this title for second year running (open women's).

1994: Played for the Canberra Breakaways, a newly formed women's rugby league team. This would be my final season playing for this rugby code. Returned to Newcastle for a third consecutive year and played in the Annual Women's Rugby Union Championship. It was requested by the ARU to "make a decision" between playing rugby union and league and commit to one code only. Selected in first Australian Women's Rugby Union International Team. Played in first International Women's Test Match, on the 2nd of September, 1994, in Sydney. ACT Wallaroos team name was transferred from Canberra Royals to Australian Rugby Union via Joan Forno.

1995: Took a break from playing "footy", both codes. Travelled to NZ to support the Australian Wallaroos in New Zealand during the second International Test in Auckland. Spectator only. Represented Port Hedland (touch football), Perth. Lots of long distance bike riding in WA included a ride to Marble Bar (Australia's hottest town). Represented Western Australia at the Annual Women's Rugby Union Championships, Canberra.

1996: Returned to Canberra for family reasons and re-signed with Royals Rugby Union Women's Team. Played in local Canberra competition, also played in Sydney women's competition as part of the Canberra Kestrels women's team. Played in Annual Women's Rugby Union Championship for Canberra (in Sydney). This was the first year of the annual tournament where only state teams were registered (as opposed to clubs). Selected in Wallaroos Squad for International Test against NZ. Played in Test Match #3 against Black Ferns and lost again. Awarded scholarship with ACT Academy of Sport. In June, played against the touring Canadian women's provincial side from Alberta.

CAREER TIMELINES

1997: Selected and played in the inaugural Women's Sevens Tournament in Hong Kong (Aussie Gold). Selected in the women's Sevens Barbarian Team (represented the Rest of the World Team) and played against Hong Kong Women's Team at Hong Kong Stadium. I scored the first try by a female athlete during this match. Retained my position in Wallaroos Squad. Founded a new Canberra women's rugby union team with Wests Rugby Union Club. Played in the first Test Match against USA Women for both ACT and Australian Wallaroo's. Took up offer with NTRU and relocated from Canberra to Darwin in preparation for 1998 World Cup.

1998: Re-located from Canberra to Darwin arriving in the Top End early January this year. I signed with South Darwin Women's Rugby Union Team. Was awarded an individual athlete scholarship with the Northern Territory Institute of Sport.

Represented NT at annual tournament for women (Darwin) for the first time. Participant in Women's Rugby World Cup Tournament (Netherlands) and played for the Australian Wallaroos. Entered powerlifting tournament for women in Darwin (won 70kg division), benching 82kg, squatting 180kg and deadlift PB 200kg and managed to retain my pelvic floor muscles.

1999: Returned to Hong Kong for second tour and as vice-captain (Aussie Gold). Continued to play for South Darwin Women's Team in the Darwin women's rugby competition. Scholarship renewed with NTIS as individual athlete. Played and trained slightly less given my commencement in the police training college. Commenced my final season of top end rugby in the women's competition. Transferred to Alice Springs for work commitment and relocated home once again.

2000: Settled into Sienna Village Accommodation, Alice Springs and commenced general duties policing. Returned to Hong Kong and participated in women's sevens international tournament for third tour (Aussie Gold). Ran with the Sydney Olympic Torch, Darwin. NTIS Scholarship renewed again. Was training with men's police rugby union team in Alice Springs.

2001: Participated in Women's Hong Kong Sevens Tournament (Aussie Gold) for fourth tour, retired from international sevens rugby. Selected in the Australian Wallaroos Squad (44 women to train for World Cup Selection). Played in international Test Matches against England (first time playing in #2 position as opposed to flanker). NTIS Scholarship renewed and funding provided for interstate and intra state travel (Sydney and Darwin) to continue maintaining match fitness and connection with national and state players. Registered with the West Harbour Sydney Women's Rugby Team in the local competition. Travelled fortnightly to Sydney to play in the NSW Women's competition during the winter season. Selected for NSW Women's State Team and played Country vs City Match for NSW (against the ACT).

2002: Selected in Australian Wallaroos team to participate in my/our second appearance as Wallaroos at this 2nd Women's Rugby Union World Cup, Barcelona, Spain (playing in the hooker role). Retired from rugby union after final game against Scotland.

HIGHLIGHTS
Women's rugby league

1991: My first game of women's rugby league will always be memorable and special. Playing for East Canberra and the ACT in 1991 and surrounded by some mates who remain lifelong friends was the beginning of a huge chapter of my young adult life.

Playing in the exhibition match at Bruce Stadium (1991) between two Canberra women's teams was a huge thrill.

1992: Being a part of the first ever ACT women's rugby league team to leave the country and represent our nation (New Zealand, 1992) was a first and in hindsight, a massive privilege. To have been awarded the "player of the day" from the ACT side during the tournament in Auckland was an honour.

Whilst on the 10-day NZ tour (Auckland) with the ACT ladies and Squizzy, one of our teammates Karen Hendricks (nicknamed Salty due the sound of her laugh) managed to assist a shop owner apprehend a young male shop lifter. A group of our team were inside a shop when the manager yelled out for assistance. Without any hesitation whatsoever, Salty tackled this Kiwi thief to the ground, allowing enough time for security to attend and restrain the offender. Salty's heroic actions made the local newspaper (it was one way of gaining publicity for our sport)!

Tracey Wilson, another great mate and champion league and union player, was mentioned in a Canberra League news article dated 8th May, 1992 (with regard to the same NZ Tour): Forward Tracey Wilson, one of the bigger girls in the squad, admitted to "feeling like a toothpick" out there, particularly after being body slammed for the first time. "None of the ACT girls can get me off the ground, "these girls didn't even raise a sweat" Wilson said.

1993: The Australian Club Championships, O'Connor Oval Canberra (July) played in the pouring rain was definitely one of the best occasions of wet, fun and muddy rugby of my playing career (which always felt better when winning)!

1999: Being selected and invited to join the Australian Jillaroos honestly was an honour but the timing just was not right for my incoming commencement in the police college.

Women's rugby union

I had the privilege of experiencing many of the "firsts" for women's rugby in Australia. I was selected in the first Australian Women's Development Squad of 1993, the first women's International Test Match on Aussie soil between Australia and New Zealand in Sydney in 1994. I was a member in the first World Cup in which the Australian Wallaroos participated in 1998, in the Netherlands. I was selected in the first tour to Hong Kong as a player in the Aussie Gold Women's Sevens Team. During this same tour, I was the first Australian female player to be invited to participate in the "Rest of the World" barbarian side to play on Hong Kong Stadium for the first time in the history of the game. Scoring that first try of that match might have been the biggest thrill in my whole playing career.

For three consecutive years, I played in the Canberra Women's Kestrels Women's Rugby Union Team. We travelled to Sydney nearly every weekend to play in the NSW women's rugby season, and for three years in a row we were victorious. Those bus trips and years spent under the coaching of Col Spence were great fun and taught me immensely.

When playing for the Canberra Kestrels in the match against Eastwood, Sydney, I became the first female player to score ten tries in one match. This was the biggest score in the history of our Kestrels team (and who knows, maybe in the NSW women's competition). Final score, Kestrels 101 – Sydney 0. No wonder I finally got tired enough and retired from rugby!

The "other" career timeline

1990: Commenced my first full time paid role out in the adult world as a "house mistress" in an English boarding school for girls in Oxford, UK. Travelled widely during this year with a backpack and push bike (after completing Yr 12 college in 1989).

1991 - 1992: Completed one year of university only (deferred study in a Bachelor of Education, Canberra) and discovered a new game called women's rugby league. Travelled to the US and drove across the country in an old Ford LTD.

1993 – 1994: Commenced basic training with Australian Protective Service, Canberra. Transferred to Port Hedland, Immigration Reception and Processing Centre, Western Australia.

CAREER TIMELINES

1995: Continued to work as an Assistance Protective Services Officer, Port Hedland.

1996: Working and travelling in Western Australia. Returned to Canberra and took leave without pay from APS while supporting family. Commenced Associate Diploma of Fitness and Recreation Leadership, Canberra Institute Technology, Bruce.

1997: Resigned from APS and continued full time studies at Tafe. Graduated with fitness and recreation leadership qualifications which set me up for next geographical move and to manage the Alawa Gym. Relocated to Darwin for Rugby World Cup preparation.

1998: Trialled for NT Police (commencement of training was deferred by 12 months due to a change in government and budget cuts) allowing me to attend the World Cup, Netherlands.

1999: Commenced basic training, NT Police College, Berrimah (Darwin) for six months. Transferred to Alice Springs before the end of this year.

2000: Shift work, Alice Springs general duties: traffic unit, domestic violence unit and juvenile task force. Played basketball in women's police team.

2001: End of probationary period as trainee constable (July). Continued to work in various departments of the Alice Springs Police Station and relief duties in remote communities at Hermannsburg and Harts Range. Short-term, high-profile case, in Criminal Investigations Branch turned my whole career 180 degrees. I headed out bush to remote community areas to work.

2002: Transferred to Yuendumu Police Station (300km west of Alice Springs) as junior member. Worked closely with Senior Aboriginal Police Officer Roy Jaburula Curtis and an absolute champion Sergeant Craig Ryan, Ric Thompson and Steve McGuire. Steep desert learning curve. Destroyed a police vehicle (Ford F250 with police cage) after hitting a cow on back road to Yuelamu. Played for Yuendumu Magpies Women's Basketball Team (and kicked butt) at annual sports weekend, winning GF against Nyrippi. Learned to speak pidgin Warlpiri (Indigenous language) and became more familiar with their culture. Absolutely loved desert life, digging for honey ants and trying bush foods for the first time.

2003: Continued to work remotely until family reasons drew me back to Canberra. Took ten months leave without pay to provide support to another young nephew and family members.

2004: Transferred to Kintore Multijurisdictional Police Station (police initiative between NT and WA) – a brand new police station built approx. 40kms from WA border, and roughly 630km west of Alice Springs in the Gibson Desert. Worked closely with Senior Police Officer Andrew Jabaltjari Spencer and two police sergeants. Attended some basic general duties and investigations training at the WA Police Academy, Perth. Sworn in as WA police constable and able to conduct police investigations on both sides of the border (NT and WA).

Established first blue light disco in these two communities. Active in youth programs to attempt to combat petrol sniffing and other youth problems. Promoted to Senior Constable. Learnt another new language, Pintubi, and thoroughly enjoyed the challenges of being an inaugural member of a brand-new police facility with Indigenous tribes, believed to be some of the last First Nations people to be located in the Australian Desert. Acquired skills in snake handling and became practiced and qualified in snake capture and release.

2005: Transferred to Ali Curung Police Station (and a bitumen road)! Promoted to Brevet Sergeant as the officer in charge of police district about the size of Victoria, Australia. Thrived in this environment alongside Senior Aboriginal Police Officer Gwen Brown. National emergency declared by prime minister (July 2005) which impacted remote work duties and life. Ran my own bi-monthly "bush court" with visiting magistrates and prosecuted my own court files. Was involved in policing and managing my first riot as police sergeant. Commenced external studies at Charles

Sturt University (BA Psychology and Sociology). Set up another branch of Blue Light Disco. Learned a million things and commenced training for Task Force trials (elite branch of NT cops). Qualified for TRG 3-day physical assessment but withdrew when subpoena arrived for the Falconio Case (Supreme Court trial) and attended court instead of trying to prove the point that a female could pass their assessment.

2006: Advised Police Superintendent (Tennant Creek) of pregnancy at about five months pregnant (feared I would be transferred if I blew the whistle too early in pregnancy). Constable Tim Fraser (champion human) sent to Ali Curung to assist with staffing while I was in the final trimester of pregnancy. Became first fully operational female Officer in Charge (while pregnant) in a remote NT community also supported by an amazing Constable Julian Laycock, another amazing cop.

2007: Three months maternity leave taken two weeks before birth of first child in Alice Springs Hospital. Became a mother and returned to operational duty in March of this year. In response to the "Little Children are sacred report" (Rex Wild QC and Patricia Anderson) Prime Minister John Howard declared a National Emergency in remote communities in the Northern Territory. These were interesting and stressful times and local Indigenous people were re-traumatised. Many changes happening.

2008: Applied for maternity leave (July) and relocated to Canberra before the birth of second child. Published my first book (Jay's Story) and distributed a copy to every remote police station in NT, every remote school and other locations and government and non-government agencies. Re-learned how to navigate Canberra roundabouts, traffic lights and supermarkets after seven years of remote life in the NT. Began building another home, south Canberra suburbs.

2009: Maternity leave without pay from NT Police. Applied to Police Commissioner to further investigate the case involving the disappearance of Peter Falconio (English backpacker who went missing in July, 2001). Offer declined and the suggestion that I "enjoy my maternity leave" resulted in my resignation from NT Police.

2010: Birth of third child at Canberra Hospital. Graduated from Charles Stuart University with Bachelor of Arts (Psychology and Sociology).

2011: Enjoying new role as full-time mother of three, supporting a partner who commenced own company, active in voluntary roles at local primary school.

2014: Birth of fourth and final child, Westmead Children's Hospital, Sydney. Commenced a brand new and challenging journey into the world of paediatric cardiology.

2015 – 2018: Life becoming super challenging while up and down from Canberra to Sydney for numerous heart and other surgeries for #4 son. In between washing, cooking, cleaning there were endless visits to our favourite places including our local zoo, Questacon, Cockington Green, our local pool for swimming lessons and Kidstart!

2019: Adjusting to single parenting and period of survival before finding a recovery program. Self-published second book (Living With Half a Heart: A Mother's Guide to Fontan Surgery) amongst enjoying local parks, bike tracks and nearby swimming holes.

2024: Self-published third book to commemorate the 30-year anniversary of the first women's rugby union Test Match on Australian soil (2nd of September, 2024). Almost time to return to paid employment and retire from full-time, stay-at-home parenting.

GLOSSARY

ARU	Australian Rugby Union
Aussie	Person of Australian heritage
Beep Test	Form of fitness testing and bloody hard work
Bugger	Aussie slang for something unpleasant or dissatisfying
Brumby	A rugby team from Canberra, Australia
Buggery	In reference to running = really fast
Burpie	Exercise done in aerobic training
Clogs	Slang term = a person from the Netherlands
Ditch	The body of water separating Australia and New Zealand (Tasman Sea)
Down Under	Another name for Australia
Ferrit	In this book refers to one of the greatest female rugby union players Kerri Louise Ferris
Footy	Rugby or Rugby union
Frog	French human
Gilbert	The ball used in a rugby union game
Honkers	Hong Kong (the country in Asia) = Aussie slang

WALLAROO #19

Humbug	Bother, bother another, annoy or pester
IRB	International Rugby Board
Kindy	Kindergarten (first year of primary schooling)
Lamo	Slang for the "lamington", iconic Australian sweet treat, made from sponge cake and traditionally coated in chocolate sauce and covered in coconut
Land down under	Australia
Libby	Nickname or short form of Elizabeth
Long white cloud	Refers to New Zealand
Mate	Friend
NTIS	Northern Territory Institute of Sport
Oz	Australia
Paddock	Playing or training field where sports are played in Australia
Pineos	Pine forest (specifically the Stromlo Pine Forest, Duffy, ACT)
Pom Bashing	Form of entertainment where Australians tease the English
Playroom	Also known as rumpus room (inside Aussie homes where children play)
Pom or Pommie	Person hailing from England or the Old Country
Pushy	Another name for bicycle or pushbike
Slang	An Australian variation or short form of the English language
Tele	Television or TV
Thingy	Something tangible

AFTERWORD

Writing this book unexpectedly taught me a lot about myself. I went back on a journey and re-visited some of the best years of my young adult life. It has been a joy and something that I wanted to tick off my bucket list. Unlocking that treasure chest which contains my folders, diaries, photo albums and programs from my rugby days brought many great memories back, including contact and catch ups with some dear old mates and coaches.

My rugby playing career was full, fun and action-packed with huge learnings in so many respects. Rugby was a priority in my life for a period of ten years; that was my choice which of course came with consequences. None of these I regret. There were good times and bad, wins and losses. The learnings from those lessons continue. These days I am on the "other side" of 50 years of age and I feel grateful for the fun, friends and love that rugby continues to bring into my life.

It is an absolute thrill to be able to sit back and watch women playing "footy" on the TV, among many other sports played at elite level and televised too. To think I played a small part in blazing this trail for the women of this century is an absolute honour. I know the best is still yet to be revealed and I look forward to playing a role in that too.

ABOUT THE AUTHOR

Libby has a background in various security roles and in policing. For about 15 years she lived and worked in remote areas of Australia undertaking work with immigration issues (Port Hedland, WA) and First Nations people (Northern Territory). She has a love of the Australian desert and the people who reside there.

Her rugby story highlights the journey of women's rugby and rugby league in Australia from 1992 – 2002. Libby shares her journey from being part of the first Australian women's rugby tournament in Newcastle 1992. She was selected in:

- The first Australian women's development team, Newcastle 1993
- The first international women's rugby international team, Sydney 1994
- The first women's Hong Kong sevens tournament, Aussie Gold 1997
- The first women's barbarian team to play on Hong Kong stadium, 1997
- The first Australian women's World Cup Wallaroos team, Amsterdam 1998.
- Australian Women's Rugby League President's team to play against the Australian National Team at ANZ Stadium, Brisbane 1999
- Jillaroos Training Squad in 1999 for the 2000 World Series Tour to Great Britian

And a whole lot more, including three additional international tours to Hong Kong playing for Aussie Gold in 1999, 2000 and 2001, and a second World Cup, Barcelona, Spain, in 2002.

Post Libby's rugby playing career, she would invest ten years of her life working in the Northern Territory Police, the majority of this period being in remote desert communities in central Australia. This career led her into motherhood which she claims has been the most challenging and rewarding thus far.

She has various qualifications in small station management, policing and a Bachelor's Degree in the Arts. She has published two other books prior to this one and enjoys good health, life, family and of course, various sports.

ACKNOWLEDGEMENTS

I would like to acknowledge women, all those who fought to be seen, heard and treated equally. I would like to also specifically acknowledge every woman who fought a battle to play the sporting code of her choice. I would like to acknowledge the pioneers of every sporting code worldwide who made it possible for Australian women to follow their lead and compete. One brave woman, somewhere in this world had to be that first one brave woman to step into the sporting arena. Thank you for following your dream and paving a new way for us all.

It became clear to me as I read widely about the journey and evolution of women, particularly sportswomen, that no matter where in the world you hail, the journey was similar and challenging yet rewarding beyond measure. It was and is definitely worth the effort and experience.

In Australia, we were ridiculed, laughed at, degraded, told we couldn't play nor had the skill to learn, provided with uniforms that were offcuts and three times the size needed to fit our smaller frames. We were told we would never play well enough to get "bums on seats" nor fill the stadium to make enough profit. We were excluded from the main arenas and playing ovals while asked to play on the back fields sometimes without even goal posts. On occasions our games were cancelled because "we didn't count" or "were not important enough". We were spat on and sworn at, teased, denied the honour of wearing our nation's colours, denied the honour of playing under our nation's title, asked to pay our own fare to represent our country, asked to return our uniforms so they could be used the following year because the budget was too tight, asked to do so many things that men would not have a clue we had to endure and just because we were born female and because we wanted to play too. Thank God those days have passed, and we continue to progress in a forward motion. There is still a way to go but I know we have proved (in so many sports and not just footy codes) that we are finally here to stay and deserve to be given a fair and equal opportunity.

Finally I thank the brave men within the ARU who made this all possible. They gave the nod from the board rooms, the old boys clubs and pubs, the coaching and players ranks and the administration desks. What a wonderful game it is and how great that we can share the joy which rugby brings to the world.

REFERENCES

Ali Donnelly (2022). *Scrum Queens: The Story of Women's Rugby*. Pitch Publishing

Barry Bowker (1976). *England Rugby; A History of the National Side, 1871-1976*. Cassell & Company Limited

CW Woodard (2021). *Queensland Women in Rugby: The First Two Years 1996-1997*. Sid Harta Books & Print Pty Ltd

Helene Joncheray (2021). *Women in Rugby*. Routledge Focus Oxon, UK.

Ian Collins & Alan Whiticker (2007). *100 Years of Rugby League. Volume 1: 1907-1966*. New Holland Publishers

Marion K. Stell (1991). *Half the Race; A History of Australian Women in Sport*. Collins Angus & Robertson

Martyn Thomas (2022). *World in their Hands: The Story of the First Women's Rugby World Cup*. Polaris Publishing Limited, Edinburgh

HONOUR ROLL

CAP NO	NAME	TOTAL CAPS
1	Karla Matua (nee Clay)	1
2	Bronwen McArthur (nee Hart)	7
3	Julie Columbus	2
4	Angel Shakespeare (nee McGurgan)	2
5	Nicole Wickert	13
6	Deena Aiken	3
7	Selena Tranter (nee Worsley)	24
8	Yasmin Muller (nee Stafford)	1
9	Louise Ferris	13
10	Helen Taylor	4
11	Sharyn Williams	1
12	Margie Brennan (nee Shelley)	1
13	Angie Doidge (nee Richards)	2
14	Kerri D Con-Goo (nee Davis)	2
15	Angie Fairweather	2
16	Ronnie May	8
17	Robyn Chambers	1

CAP NO	NAME	TOTAL CAPS
18	Tina Chapman	1
19	Elizabeth Andrew	12
20	Bronwyn Calvert	8
21	Kathryn Beitzel	1
22	Vicky Botterell	2
23	Pearl Kaleopa-Palaialii	14
24	Lisa-Jane Dwan	9
26	Shirley Russell	5
27	Meredith Bochmann	1
28	Karen Lambert	1
29	Carmel Brennan (nee Davoren)	1
30	Jane Hamilton	1
31	Louise Barron	2
32	Christine Henson	6
33	Rebecca Cleary (nee Wakim)	10
34	Mieke Fortune (nee Gladwin)	10
35	Gail Barlow	1
36	Sharon O'Kane	15
37	Tanya Osborne	10
38	Cathy Boulton	1
39	Naomi Roberts (nee Ragogo)	11
40	Vanessa Bradley (nee Nooteboom)	8
41	Leanne Matthewson (nee Wilkes)	1

HONOUR ROLL

CAP NO	NAME	TOTAL CAPS
42	Helen Langley (nee Theunissen)	8
43	Sherilee Moulds	6
44	Bronwyn Mackintosh	14
45	Karen Bucholz	2
46	Perise Ili	7
47	Tui Ormsby	24
48	Bronwyn Laidlaw	10
49	Melissa Latu-Lutui	12
50	Holly Birch	4
51	Jennifer Williams	3
52	Melanie Goehr	2
53	Genevieve Delves	3
54	Kristy Frogley	1
55	Debbie Grylls	1
56	Anita Carlin	1
57	Penelope Anderson	6
58	Alena Summers	2
59	Lisa Fiaola	13
60	Nyree Osieck	5
61	Louise Burrows (nee Cooke)	22
62	Jennifer Egan	6
63	Paige Butcher	5
64	Cheryl McAfee (nee Soon)	21
65	Charmain Stevenson (nee Smith)	5
66	Davina Kruger (nee Craft)	3

WALLAROO #19

CAP NO	NAME	TOTAL CAPS
67	Ianthe Astley-Boden	3
68	Jamie Blazejewski	4
69	Alyssa Campbell	3
70	Alex Hargreaves	17
71	Debby Carley (nee Hodgkinson)	9
72	Lindsay Morgan	14
73	Alicia Frost	7
74	Kate Porter	12
75	Kim Wilson	8
76	Tasileta Bethell	9
77	Rachelle Pirie	2
78	Tricia Brown	21
79	Rebecca Anderson	5
80	Ruan Sims	9
81	Tobie McGann	12
82	Silei Poluleuligaga	13
83	Se'ei Sa'u	10
84	Rebecca Smyth (nee Trethowan)	15
85	Chris Ross	13
86	Kelli Donnelly	4
87	Iliseva Batibasaga	26
88	Alana Thomas	7
89	Lee Kenny (nee Fata)	2
90	Annette Finch	1
91	Tegan French	1

HONOUR ROLL

CAP NO	NAME	TOTAL CAPS
92	Cassandra Bailey (nee Nunn)	2
93	Megan Valler	2
94	Kylie Pennell	5
95	Louise Morrison	3
96	Dalena Dennison	8
97	Nicole Beck	8
98	Sharni Smale (nee Williams)	23
99	Selene Sheerin (nee Thornton)	2
100	Danielle Meskell	12
101	Melissa Armstrong (nee Rowe)	2
102	Margaret Watson	13
103	Cobie-Jane Morgan	20
104	Kristy Giteau	5
105	Ashleigh Hewson	18
106	Rebecca Clough	24
107	Emerena Marsh-Aviga (nee Marsh)	1
108	Caroline Fairs (nee Vakalahi)	9
109	Shannon Parry	24
110	Cheyenne Campbell	17
111	Megan Shanahan	1
112	Stacey Kilmister	2
113	Chloe Butler	14
114	Mollie Gray	13
115	Natasha Haines	9
116	Alisha Hewett	21

WALLAROO #19

CAP NO	NAME	TOTAL CAPS
117	Ashley Marsters	28
118	Nita Maynard	7
119	Hanna Sio	8
120	Liz Patu	33
121	Brooke Saunders	3
122	Oneata Schwalger	7
123	Alexandra Sulusi	3
124	Kenina Terita	2
125	Michelle Milward	8
126	Madeline Putz	3
127	Hayley Barclay	1
128	Michelle Perry	2
129	Angela Hipwell	2
130	Ivy Kaleta	2
131	Nareta Marsters	9
132	Hana Ngaha	11
133	Sarah Riordan	10
134	Shontelle Stowers	1
135	Vesinia Schaaf-Taufa	3
136	Emily Robinson	24
137	Katrina Barker	9
138	Ariana Kaiwai	1
139	Alanna Patison	2
140	Grace Hamilton	29
141	Kirby Sefo	2
142	Chloe Leaupepe	1

HONOUR ROLL

CAP NO	NAME	TOTAL CAPS
143	Michelle Bailey	1
144	Evelyn Horomia	7
145	Victoria Latu	3
146	Fenella Hake	10
147	Kayla Sauvao	8
148	Ashleigh Timoko	3
149	Huia Swannell	2
150	Samantha Treherne	14
151	Kiri Lingman	5
152	Hilisha Samoa	7
153	Millie Boyle	12
154	Violeta Tupuola	4
155	Trilleen Pomare	27
156	Mahalia Murphy	18
157	Kate Brown	2
158	Emily Chancellor	23
159	Georgia O'Neill	2
160	Crystal Maguire	2
161	Atasi Lafai	12
162	Mhicca Carter	6
163	Shanice Parker	2
164	Alice Tonumaivao	1
165	Darryl Wickliffe	2
166	Melissa Fatu	2
167	Averyl Mitchell	4
168	Michaela Leonard	25

WALLAROO #19

CAP NO	NAME	TOTAL CAPS
169	Ariana Hira-Herangi	4
170	Alysia Lefau-Fakaosilea	4
171	Asoiva Karpani	24
172	Lori Cramer	21
173	Georgia Cormick	3
174	Shannon Mato	4
175	Arabella McKenzie	24
176	Christina Sekona	3
177	Alana Elisaia	5
178	Georgina Friedrichs	22
179	Kaitlan Leaney	18
180	Bridie O'Gorman	20
181	Pauline Piliae-Rasabale	11
182	Adiana Talakai	16
183	Ivania Wong	15
184	Madison Schuck	7
185	Piper Duck	13
186	Sera Naiqama	13
187	Jemima McCalman	4
188	Layne Morgan	22
189	Annabelle Codey	5
190	Cecilia Smith	13
191	Tiarna Molloy	1
192	Grace Kemp	6
193	Bree-Anna Cheatham	9
194	Siokapesi Palu	9

HONOUR ROLL

CAP NO	NAME	TOTAL CAPS
195	Bienne Terita	5
196	Maya Stewart	11
197	Tania Naden	13
198	Carys Dallinger	6
199	Faitala Moleka	9
200	Tabua Tuinakauvadra	6
201	Jasmin Huriwai	6
202	Leilana Nathan	5
203	Brianna Hoy	6
204	Desiree Miller	5
205	Sarah Dougherty	2
206	Melanie Wilks	1
207	Samantha Wood	3
208	Sally Fuesaina	3
209	Hera-Barb Malcolm Heke	3
210	Caitlyn Halse	2

On this celebration of 30 years since our first international women's rugby union Test Match, played on the 2nd of September, 1994, at North Sydney Oval, I congratulate every Australian Wallaroo. I further congratulate every coach, manager, doctor, physiotherapist and all support staff who played their role for every team during this period. Special thanks also go to the Australian Rugby Union and all state and territory unions around this amazing country. Cheers and thank you.

Wallaroos Caps above were current as of 29th of June, 2024. Special thanks to Jilly Collins, General Manager, Women's Rugby, Rugby Australia Ltd for providing this updated list and for the work you continue to undertake for women's rugby.

www.ingramcontent.com/pod-product-compliance
Lightning Source LLC
Chambersburg PA
CBHW020406080526
44584CB00014B/1188